BEYOND *the* BORDERS

Of Questions and Offerings

Shakya Sen

PARTRIDGE
A Penguin Random House Company

To order additional copies of this book, contact
Partridge India
000 800 10062 62
www.partridgepublishing.com/india
orders.india@partridgepublishing.com

CONTENTS

THE OMNIPRESENCE

In the serenity of the universe
Signaling the advent of the dawn
As a prelude to the earth's welcome
To a charming new-born morn,
Awe-filled, as my soul I bare,
I find that You are there.

As the sun rises in the upper skies
And throws its scorching heat around
And sucks the water from the oceans
And sets on fire, the earthly ground,
While I thirst for peace with none to care,
I find that You are there.

As the sun leans towards the West
To set, and the twilight zone
Engulfs the world with a host of colours
From sources yet unknown,—
Before my eyes a wink could spare,
I find that You are there.

In the constant spell of my tragic moments
Through days and months and years
As I burden myself with the aftermath
Which a ravaged destiny bears,
In the shape of melancholy, grief and despair,
I find that You are there.

In happy hours of my life
When I lift myself from the vile
And see a reason which for a moment
Allows me to smile,—
Amidst the laughter and fanfare,
I find that You are there.

When I hate someone and cannot stand
His presence 'fore my eyes,
And his entire bearing in every form
Seems to me to be filled with vice,
While my wrath and hatred charge the air,
I find that You are there.

When I love a woman of my dreams
And feel her magic charms
And taste and sense my virile pleasures
And hold her in my arms,
In the ecstasy of love and passion which we share,
I find that You are there.

As I travel through life's diverse stations
Loading my mortal existence
With so much to see, to feel and to absorb
With my limited human sense,
While I spread the cream of life on every new-found layer,
I find that You are there.

And the day when I shall reach
The last of all my destinations
And bid my last goodbye
As I leave the last of all the stations,
When Death shall beckon and shall stare,
I'll find that You are there!

THE MAGIC

My pains have transformed themselves into
A realisation of an art
Where my soul is painted with the words:
"Thou art, Lord, Thou art!"
From whatever source my spirit soars
High above all mortal grounds,
Your image in its pristine glory
Makes its quiet graceful rounds.
In me, I find Your presence ensured,
In me, I hear Your call;
In me, I've stored Your affections,
Your love, adorations and all.
In You, I have my confidence
Reposed since my birth;
In You, my mortal entity
Has found its divine worth.
From whichever angle I view this life,
Either through You or me,
Our merger makes me a complete man
In fullness and entirety.
Life then finds its winsome meaning
Through every step of mine
In my voyage towards the destined unknown
In search of the superfine,
While I'll be left with nothing but
Peace and peace alone
In realms spread out far and near,
Whether known or yet unknown.
And the artwork realised through my pains
Playing their divine role,
Shall be the essence of the magic
Woven in my soul.

A FRIEND

Divinity descends to befriend me

When all have parted ways

And holds my arms in quiet embrace

And plants kisses on my face.

That's when I could sense in me

The greatest pleasure ever

And wish to hold her in my grips

Forever and forever.

That's when I could discard all

That's worldly and not lasting

With the touch of divinity wrapping me

In happiness everlasting.

That's where the markings of my life

Howsoever ill-fated,

In the touch of divine class, do stand

Totally obliterated.

Nothing remains to be wished for further

In the span of my existence

As divinity settles in me to calm

My mortal turbulence.

THE INVITATION

These moments, when I'm all alone

Idling away my time,

Seem to be priceless with their silence

Balancing my living rhyme.

Here my ceaseless lusts for life

Are transformed into peace

To spend my time-bound breathing hours

With soulful ease.

In recognition of your magnitude

Simply by staring at your sky,

And in endless search for your identity,

My obmutescent prayers lie.

With countless thoughts which lead to you,

My emptiness is filled;

And in the wilderness of a forlorn life,

My rues are stilled.

Nothing more is precious than

Your links which tend to seal

My destined grief and distress which

Hardly seem to heal.

Let me therefore be alone

With a silent invitation

To you to enter in my soul

And find your seat and station.

THE PRIVACY

In the world of men where everyone

Shall stay and leave alone,

I've nothing to grieve and nothing to repent

For a feeling that's not my only own.

I know as much as you do know

That in the hearts of all of us,

We've reserved a space for ourselves only

Through which we can ourselves pass.

That's not a place where all can enter,

That's not a space which we can share,

But that's a private corner which

Prohibits others' thoroughfare.

There we survive all alone

Exclusively with our joy and tears,

With our wreckage and trophies unrecognised

And unsung in open public spheres.

THE FEEL OF FORTIFICATION

Breathless, I stand with trembling feet

On devastations across the earth

And try to assess the worth and reason

Of man's ignoble birth.

In the magnitude of thoughts which are,

Or should be, good and pure,

Is this what man endlessly

Through ageless time endure?

In the melee of these destructions

Rampant everywhere,

The goodness of man's artistry

Is lost in the poisoned air.

Our endeavour to extract even

A speck of purity from

The toxicity thus spread by man

Through the noxious ruinous storm,

Shall be welcomed by the ravaged millions

Wrecked in the hellish fire

Stripped of shelter, food and health

'Midst the devil's great bonfire;

And existence shall be fortified

Even by the feel

That someone's waiting with the balm

Whether it does or does not heal.

THE SYMPHONY

If the violent strength of the thunderstorm

Raging through this night,

Could force its entry in my soul

And wash away my baneful plight,

The rupture caused by the forceful access

Would act as my finest balm

To provide all that's needed to

Usher in my peace and calm.

The wild and untamed gate-crash shall

Perforce help to bring a state

To counter and to drive out deftly

My wild and untamed fate.

Blow, therefore, ah, blow with fury,

And raise that mighty force

Which the wind can carry crossing limits

To break open all my sensual doors.

For in the ruins and devastations

I'll perceive

The much sought freedom of my soul

In this thunderstorm-filled eve.

In the ravage that shall be left behind,

I'll slowly search and find

My union with the divine goodness

And my final peace of mind.

And my soul shall lie in symphony

And perfectly orchestrated

With the furious sounds of the heavens where

All others are outdated.

A REQUEST

As I stand alone in the wilderness

Of existence and life

Where fate has unduly sworn

Ruin and devastation, I only pray

> Let me simply be
>
> On my own!

While roaming alone through endless tracts

In futile search of peace,

Where no harvest has been reaped, no crop has grown,

My only solace shall be if you

> Let me simply be
>
> On my own!

Where nothing seems to match my mind

And I am yet to find a friend so true,

In a world where I am left alone,

The passwords to my comfort are:

> Let me simply be
>
> On my own!

In the massive network of what's called 'life',

Where I have found my solitary ground

Built on a cracking stone,

In the chaos and disorder, 'Sturm und Drang',

> Let me simply be
>
> On my own!

In the cravings of a life which has gone astray

Through hopeless hours spent in vain,

With a thousand reasons to quietly mourn

In the graveyard of my buried hopes,

> Let me simply be
>
> On my own!

In the star-studded presentation of the mortal world

Immortalising the fancied dreams of man,

There's not a single grain I own

Save and except my soulful wish:

> Let me simply be
>
> On my own!

Across the debris of life where my footfalls leave

Marks of blood which oozes from

An existence quite out of tone,

Through my onward journey in search of God,

> Let me simply be

> On my own!

As I wait in anxious anticipation

In course of my tedious walk of life,

Of the welcome arms of a friend unknown

When I shall cross my mortal border,

> Let me simply be

> On my own!

THE EXPECTATION

And the devil speaks to me

In God's counterfeited tone

And ushers in chaos and restlessness

In my living zone.

And the more I'm convinced of the words

Which the devil spells aloud,

The more I feel the mess and nuisance

In life's great roundabout.

Such are the devil's words which make

My present glories shine

And create a dreamland of my own

And treat it to be mine.

Oblivious of all that are

Preached by God so long,

The devil's wishes gain their strength

And support what is wrong.

In the melodrama of what is known as life,

I walk the goddamned path

Ignorant of the massacre

Which waits in its aftermath.

But when this life shall end itself

With all its ruinous past,

I know, I know, You shall come

To carry me at last!

<u>Who Unto Him Rules</u>

My existence must twine its roots

Deep within that of Yours

To ensure that we fructify

With the pains that life endures.

In whatever way You may then choose

To define or redefine

My life in pains, the pleasure shall

Be mine and only mine.

Pains have always been the cause

Of giving birth to pleasure,

As adventure in our existence

Is the root to find the treasure.

Shorn of pains and despondency

And bereft of all thunderstorms,

The art of life would have no meaning

Nor would hunt for finer forms.

That's the reason why the stars

Seem bright and graceful in the dark

And silence seems so grand and peaceful

After the end of the blaring bark.

That's the reason why a man born blind

Exults on gaining sight;

And sacrifice for a needful cause,

Fills the void inside.

That's the reason why You and I

In fragrance blossom alike,

In the midst of my human pains and tears

When acute tragedies strike.

THE ATTEMPT

The rains have stopped but my lawn is wet

And the air is cool and soothing now

And the earth is quiet and peaceful after

Violent nature's stormy row.

My world is likewise quiet and peaceful

After the raging fatal storms

Have washed away all aspirations

To leave me with my own reforms.

The storms have stopped but my eyes are wet

And my life is cool and soothing though,

While I give in to my fate's dictates

And the sombre traits are felt no more.

But as much as I would like to step

Forward on my own

By reforming myself with the future,

Yet I find it hard to disown

The memories left behind

Which unduly, as obsessions, adhere

To every move I make

With an immense burden to cheerfully bear

The forward march in life

By detaching myself from the pains

While I look behind and try to forget

The past remains.

THE THRUST

The dawn with the touch of its shimmering lights

Is a feast for my mortal eyes

Where You stand and spray Your cosmic rays

And the Godly waves arise

To reveal the beauty and the peace

Latent in every man

And every speck in the universe

Which my soul can bear to scan.

Here then lies the superb articulation

Of Divinity through the ages

Exulting in their awesome splendour

Through the majesty of Your images

Laid out everywhere in the chaos

Characterised as life

Where nothing without Your strength and order

Can exist or survive.

Whatever sins I have accumulated

And whatever goodness gained,

Disappear into nothingness while I

Am left alone and drained

Of all my earthly longings where

My emancipation lies

In my rendezvous with You this dawn

Where You arise

While darkness quits and provides room

For the entry of Your lights

And thrusts me into Your royal abode

Of mystic delights!

THE CALL

As evening descends and the day departs

With heavy, weary strides,

A sort of gloom now engulfs me

As I think of all my tired rides

Across the undulations of my life

And the passages I have crossed

In course of which my strength and patience

Have both been somewhere lost.

As the evening slowly gives in to

The darkness of the night,

Depression with its heavy burden

Enhances my fatigue and my fright.

Life seems void of all its meaning,

My spirit seems to dry

As I see myself as a wreck of a man

Left alone to cry.

Throughout the wretched nightly hours,

Sleeplessness solely reigns

While aspirations disappear into nothingness

And their skeletons remain—

Till the hour when the night gives way

To the advent of the dawn

And the horizon shimmers with the light

To give birth to an early morn.

And that's the hour when Your Godhead

Works wonders in my all

Where my despair, fatigue and hopelessness

Vanish while You call!

THE SEARCH

My despairs are but constellations

In hope's unreachable sky

Where, in the cosmic galaxies,

Your unattainable images lie.

And as I proceed to hurl with joy

Hopelessness's masterpieces

In the vastness of Your universe,

My ardent psychic wishes

Find their fulfilment where You

Exist with Your divine powers

Ruling as the King of Kings

Over all my given destined hours.

And that's the charm of life and living

As I search for You along

The painful bleeding path where all

My trepidations throng

Like stars clustered in the Milky Way

To produce the whitish glow

Likened to the shimmering hopes

Where the stars of despairs find no show.

THE SELECTION

My physique basked in the warmth of Satan

And my soul basked in that of God

While destiny with its storm and thunder

Ran rough-shod

Over life and my existence

Breathing fire

To prepare, as if, my extermination

On the burning pyre.

What if I feel revolting

Against God and Satan, both?

And create history to be rewritten

By a daring anecdote?—

The anecdote of death in life

And life in death—

Where the twain who shall never meet,

Will be found to have met?

Where life meets death

And death meets life,

Where the fusion is so mighty

That the elements of both survive,—

Where the darkness of the devil

Merges with celestial lights

Where the infernal dungeons merge

With heavenly heights—

Where war and hatred

Give ample way

To peace and love

All the way,—

At that point of amalgamation

Of the evil and the good,

On the relics of devastation,

Stands God, as God has always stood.

No more shall the physique bask

In the warmth of Satan then,

As the soul shall bask in that of God

As the saviour of all men.

A FRIEND

Through my lifelong wait, I've not yet met

A quiet friend: his name is Death.

And he shall some day lift his veil

And invite me to set my sail

After exhaling my last living breath.

Thus I shall wait for him to turn

To me when I will have my turn

To speak alone to him and wholly

Find a mate to confide solely

Before I unto my source return.

In him I shall my freedom find

From the shackles of the earth behind

And reach my long sought goal

Through the unbound ecstasy of the soul

Unleashed in eternity and well-defined.

I shall therefore never die

But find a newer life. Yes I

Shall exist in the elements

Without the mortal scars and dents

In the levels where I'll lie.

THE EXPECTATION

Am I to find my emancipation

Through the workload You have thrust

On me till I clear the massive burden

Before I am reduced into dust?

With tired limbs and trudging feet,

I am yet to find my final rest,

While weariness now finds in me

It's flamboyant nest.

What carries me is not my physique

But my will to cross the miles

Spread ahead through unknown hurdles

Before I close my mortal files.

Uncertainties do haunt me always

But the certainty of death

Ushers in the strength and power

To clear the burden of my debt

Which I owe to life and existence

In every shape and form

And withstand the lashing effects of

This ongoing thunderstorm.

I've convinced myself that soon the storm

Shall be over and the calm

Following it shall fetch my rest

In Your welcome arm!

At St. John's Church, Kolkata

Here I stand today as if

The chronicles of the bygone

Resurrect themselves 'fore my senses

Irretrievably drawn

From all that's ancient, priceless and

Bedecked with the charms

Lent to them through age-long splendours

In time's ageless arms.

Every breath of air inhaled

Through the breathless hours spent

Ushers in a thrilling feeling

Where the past and the present blend.

Time has bred it's elegance

On the relics of the past

Where antiquity's magnificence

Remains splendour-cast.

If history begins with all that had

Been once upon a time,

The curiosity to explore the forgotten

Tastes sublime.

Moments such as these have enthralled

My entire heart and mind

To feel the vibrations through my present

Of the timelessness behind.

Mortality must bow in awe

Where immortality loftily stands

And man with his ancient wisdom,

The Godly understands,

The realisation of which

Ripens and lends

Celestial divinity

To my mortal existence.

WHERE?

In a torn and shredded world where life

Stands amidst a raging war,

In quest of peace, I search the rubble

And stare aghast in awe

At the devil's agents who taint and stab

Humanity from the back

While in futility I look for reasons

In the mayhem's huge haystack.

Once upon a glorious time

When each of us was born,

The innocence of the child in us

Was bestowed on each to adorn

Our lives like a sparkling jewel

Resembling the priceless goodness of a child,

Only to be wasted henceforth

And be disastrously defiled.

And in the blasts of poison, you and I

Through adverse currents, stand to bear

The brunt of the catastrophe

And the ignoble atmosphere.

Where's the divine omnipotence

To ordain a complete ban

On the self-destructive plenipotence

Of a living demon called man?

Celebrate Life!

Celebrate life

In details.

Gently lift

All the veils

Around you

Which unduly shroud

Your visions with the density

Of a stagnant cloud.

By this you will

And must have found

The vibrating colours

Of life around.

Colours which include

Both black and white,

Features which project

Both the dark and bright.

In the realisation of reality,

All your doubts

Shall fade. And existence's

Whereabouts

Shall be revealed

To untie the knots

To enter into the Book of Wisdom

Prepared by the Gods.

THE FINAL INSPIRATION

Where opulence has a strong foothold

And luxury comes to stay,

Fold your hands in prayers to

Let peace find its way.

Carve a niche in every corner

To place your spirit's thoughts

Of all that's peaceful, all that's blissful

And join the displaced dots

Scattered through a life of plenty

Where destiny has cruelly barred

The healing of the wounds and despairs

Which still lie badly scarred.

In every child here, you shall find

Your love displayed;

In every life on earth, you'll see

Your passions spread

Their caring wings to fetch you joy

Unfathomable throughout—

And that indeed, so unhesitatingly,

Is what life is all about!

The tears you shed then, shall form themselves

Into drops of gold

Much needed to soulfully sympathise

Where poverty has its hold.

Wherever in the vastness of this world

You may seek to tread,

Your affections shall be remembered in glory

And be always marked as read.

And that shall always be the source

Of the inspiration to live

In peace in a world of affluence

With the urge to gift and give.

DISCRIMINATION

My pleasure mixes with my grief

And raises unique notes

Of strange music through my soul

With unseen heavy loads

To weigh me down with thoughts galore

To question why

Should there be this discrimination

Between You and I:

The discrimination as to why there should

Be reasons enough to feel

That God is great and man is lowly

Through every blasted deal;

The discrimination that omnipotence

Rests in God alone;

That the words of God are sacrosanct

And those of man's, error-prone;

The discrimination that destiny shall

Only be applicable

To the life of man, where God shall be

Exempted from the table;

The discrimination that Gods shall rule

And man shall always serve;

That Gods shall always find the pleasures

Of Paradise, while man shall deserve

His place on earth with pains and agony

To perish, waste and rot

And remain satisfied with whatever little

Fate should or should not allot;

And alas, also, the discrimination

That Gods can never lie

And unlike man, should live forever

And can never die.

And thus my pleasure finds its way

Through my grief's wailing walls

Where I find my wisdom stays afloat

Despite Your frantic calls.

THE DISTINCTION

With heavy eyelids filled with sleep

I can't write even a line or two

While all my thoughts just rush together

To reach the crossroad of the false and true

And make a mess of the thoroughfare

Where sleep and awakening lie

With the frantic effort to distinguish

The divine 'You' from my mortal 'I'.

And that is how my living hours

Are spent to strike a balance 'tween

All that can be seen in life

And the rest that can't be seen.

And through this endless contradiction,

I try to find out, if I at all can,

The subtle joint at the junction of

The godly devil and the lowly man.

My mind is bound, my tongue is tied

With knots of untruth, while

The madman speaks out all that's true

Without pausing even for a while.

In the darkness of the space beyond

Knowledge, wisdom and understanding,

The streak of light which casts its glow

Is your eternal omnipotent standing

In the protection of the true and the false;

Of wisdom and folly; of the seen and the unseen;

Of sleep and awakening; of the godly and the lowly;

Of all that are and all that once have been.

THE BLENDING

Music sounds its beats in me

As poetry travels through

The senses of my grief and pleasure

Deftly set by You.

Through many a grand and charming cycle

Of light and darkness, both,

Like the superb magic of a charmer,

My life has stayed afloat.

Just where I've been pierced with pains

By the pointed needle of your dart,

I feel the magnitude of the contrast

In happiness, when happiness fills my heart.

My joy and sorrow, both are blended

With poetry into one

Where they match themselves in a game of contrasts

And my life's lessons are done.

In the fascinating world of survival

Through colours, both black and white,

I've mixed them with red and green and blue and all

Without setting them aside.

And a fantastic mix then shows itself

Like a rainbow in the sky

Where I absorb all my pleasure, all my grief

To lift me ever high

And higher at the levels where

You and Your divinity lie

In the massive unfathomed universe

Where we can merge together—You and I!

Ancient Regime

Far beyond all mortal bondage,

Someday I shall find my home

To rest my soul once and for all

At the elevation where you roam.

My grief shall transform itself into

Worship and prayers while

My happiness from its selfish nature

Shall unconditionally resile.

And cleansed of all my emotions

And feelings which I hold,

In course of the tryst with You, O Lord,

I shall then behold

Myself as a part of You

From whom my soul was long back drawn

To travel through the earthly lives

Since the advent of its dawn.

Let this therefore be the last

Of lives which I have spent on earth;

Let Your dictum be now lifted

On rebirth,

So that I may leave the world

With the final peace of mind

That the sword shall no more hang on me

Of the divine mastermind;

So that once again I may merge with You

And regain my ancient power

Through divine omnipotence from the source whereof

I gained my life at the first natal hour.

THE BLOSSOMING

As I indulge myself in the sweetness of

Solitude at its best

And smear myself with the passing breeze

In divine-flavoured zest,

My entire bearing finds its meaning

Stretched out 'fore my eyes

And dissolves itself in the massive space

Across the star-studded skies.

Here I lose the sense of being

A mortal on this earth,

While immortality from some unseen range

Sounds its first alert;

As if through the stints of life

Moving from the bad to worse,

My soul and spirit find their freedom

In the magnificence of the universe.

I sink with the burden of my life

Into dungeons down and deep

And heave, as I sway with You beside,

A sigh of great relief.

This, for me, is a way of life,

And a way of death as well,

Where You and I in matching contrast

With eternal pleasure dwell;

Where You lose Yourself in my spirit

And I, in Your massive power,

And both of us, within each other

Find reasons to flourish and to flower.

The Perfection of Life

Life stands before me with all its glamours

And strikes an untamed pose

Like an undressed maiden in the wild

Face to face with me and close.

And as I rush to touch her contours

And hold her in my grips

Through the game of 'touch me now and touch me not',

The image somehow slips

Out of control, but the charm,

The scent, the feeling and the sense

Of the gratifying moments through the will-o-the-wisp

Of life commence.

And through my exhaustion and depression,

She beckons me again with the same game-plan,

And I rise again with renewed vigour

And rush to grasp her like a love-stung man.

My frenzy lends me the virile strength

To unravel life's deepest interiors

And feel the marvel and the beauty

Which the lovely lady bears.

And after all these years are spent

By holding life in my human arms,

She'll disclose herself in another form—

Death—as one of her sundry other charms.

And my union with life with all her wonders

Shall be then complete

With the fullest perfection through chaos and turmoil

Of my lifelong mortal feat.

THE DISCARDMENT

Let me dance away through time

Holding life in one hand

And death in another

And understand

The charms of both

And kiss them in turns

As each, after its own span

Of time, unto me returns.

As I kiss life, let me feel

Her undulating curves

And press her hard to seek and explore

The pleasures my soul deserves.

Let me search her nooks and corners

And find her virgin spots

And taste her entire fabric through

All the evens and the odds—

Till death, the other maiden pulls

Me away from life to lie lovelocked

And taste her texture all alone

With the weird stories she has stocked.

Let me therefore feel the curves

Of virgin death, just as I

Have felt the curves of life with pleasure,

Without heaving a single sigh.

With both the maidens—life and death—

I shall play the game

Of love and kisses all throughout

Till each of them in turn shall claim

My soul, till my soul

By itself shall discard

Both life and death as useless partners

In time's endless chart.

THE FINAL SAY

Beyond the periphery of today

Where tomorrow awaits its birth

Through the unknown span of time

Circling around the girth

Of existence and life,

I seek to cast my vision

And explore the mystery and the awe

In the cryptic world where the future hides

Its claws within its padded paw.

And thus I strive

Within the limited boundary of today

To eradicate and erase

Despair as the lurking trespasser

In the melodrama within the maze

Created by my fate.

And by the time when I should cross

The boundary line of today

And step into the world of the unknown tomorrow

And prepare myself for the day,

I shall not hate My Creator, for by then

I shall have mustered the strength

To survive through the future

By having meaningfully spent

My hours today.

And someday in the future when

The grand invitation from Divinity

Shall be delivered to me for merging myself

With Eternity,

I shall have the final say!

SONG OF DEATH

Stop your haughty strides and glance
At me for a moment much 'fore I
Block your way and confront you,
Hey Life! You ignorant passer-by!

Greet me once and greet me often
For then I shall not deny
Your existence till you exhaust yourself,
Hey Life! You ignorant passer-by!

Understand my whims and fancies
And treat me as a close ally,
For I shall grant you emancipation,
Hey Life! You ignorant passer-by!

Strange as it sounds, yet I shall never
Let you down or lie
In the matter of our tryst in the future
Hey Life! You ignorant passer-by!

You shall find your grand relief
From your greatest pain or saddest sigh
Through me alone at the ordained hour,
Hey Life! You ignorant passer-by!

Believe in me as you take your strides
Along earthly undulations, low and high,
And you'll have nothing to fear through the arduous trek,
Hey Life! You ignorant passer-by!

Merge yourself with eternity where I
Roam alone, and you shall not die
Even in death where we shall be one,
Hey Life! You ignorant passer-by!

From me you shall learn to remove
All hallucinations which lie
Scattered around man's existence,
Hey Life! You ignorant passer-by!

In me you shall find your genesis
And the eternal bondage and the tie
Through the countless lives you lived before,
Hey Life! You ignorant passer-by!

I shall stand as your only friend
When you shall say your last goodbye;
I shall aid your resurrection and immortality,
Hey Life! You ignorant passer-by!

<u>YOUR DIVINITY</u>

In the silence of the darkness here,

I find my unseen friend

Concealed in my surroundings

Which seem to quietly blend

With the lust and desire of my soul

To be one with Your sole entity

In the mystic cryptic realm where

My friend is Your Divinity.

I'll roam around now hand in hand

With Divinity by my side

And in glory, I shall love her gently

And embrace her inside.

I'll crave for her in life and death,

And till the last day of eternity

For I have found my friend in her:

My darling in Your Divinity!

<u>The True Meaning</u>

As I surf the channels of my life

And try to find out where has this

Life of mine through its onward course

Intermittently gone amiss,

I draw a blank, for every channel seems

To show me colours endlessly

Of all that's charming, all that's godly,

Of all that's yet to be!

I've exposed my inner self this day

And found my outer home

In the world of sunshine spread throughout

The vastness where you roam.

Your presence makes its presence felt

In the fragrance in the breeze

Which lifts me up with gentle motions

With pleasures such as these.

My existence seems blessed now

With divinity in the lead

Where nothing seems to have gone amiss

And nothing seems to bleed.

Nothing in life could have ever been

More well-defined;

No pain could have ever tainted life

In its history left behind.

Whatever could carry the meaning of

Life in its truest sense,

Lies inextricably merged in oneness with

My entire mortal existence.

THE ULTIMATE AWARD

Day by day I've learnt my lessons

While travelling through my pains

Of being left alone in a crowded world

Where nothing of me remains.

Each day is, by itself, a

Reminder of the times

Spent in blasts of undue grief

Or in charming rhymes.

Each morning dawns with hopes anew

As the sunrays return to light

The world and lift it from

The darkness to my delight.

But despair sets in when all hopes

Lie unfulfilled through the days

And wreck my worldly aspirations

Through life's chequered plays.

The sunshine then has just no meaning

Where devastation wraps

Life from all its nooks and corners

And hopelessness lends its awry gaps.

The world mayn't be, but I am tired

Of playing this awful game

Of retrieving a hope from life's debris

And then being deprived of it again.

But should I hold this state of life

As my grandest mortal game

Where Divinity with all its glory, blossoms

Through the severity of my pain?

THE CONVERSION

I hardly ever understand

The source from which I draw

My strength through pains and sufferings,

Rawest of the raw.

When fate is a rapier piercing through

My entity within,

Where, not blood, but my entire existence

Oozes in the din,

I find the chance to marvel at

The superpower which ensconced lies

In You, from which I draw a fractioned speck

To relive my life before it dries.

From the blasts, a few, of hurt and pain,

Oceans of wellness soar

Where I find my access ensured where

I am in me no more.

And as my entity stretches itself

Beyond the barriers of my 'I',

The vacuum in me sucks in all

The marvels which mystify

My soul with the language which You speak,

The sparkle with which You shine,

To celebrate on earth, the merger of

The worldly with the divine.

My agonies are then transformed into

The finest pleasures, which then seem

To fetch my peace and calm within

Which had so long, dormant been.

THE QUESTION

While the river Ganges on its own,

Flows with silent motions,

Oblivious of the world around

And all our human notions,

Love and hate lie scattered along

The extents of its banks

With all that's lovely, all that's ugly

Showing on its flanks.

At places I have reasons to

Taste a piece of peace,

While elsewhere the taste of life is sour

Where hate prepares the crease.

I find it hard to find out where

This contrast has its source

And who must be the unknown spoilsport

To taint the unspoilt course;

Is it man or is it God, or both combined

Who must somewhere take the blame

And share the penalty slapped on him

For playing this awful game?

Unto whom shall humanity

Ever so explicitly relate,

This timeless eternal saga

Of love and hate?

(At Millenium Park, Kolkata)

SONG OF THE CORPSE

I'm here to search for peace in life

Through the chronicles of the dead

And to find my final comfort zone

In the earth-filled silent bed.

Death here is the host which welcomes

Life in the dinner-dance

At the end of all the lifelong turmoil

For the once-in-a-lifetime chance

Of a raw encounter with my Maker

In confidence and trust

Through the long journey of emancipation

Ending with the dust.

But even here I've got to still

Await my resurrection

Into the world of life on the judgment day

After God's great vivisection.

Swaying between the world of mortals

And the world of immortality,

My soul is yet to merge in oneness

With the span of eternity.

Life beyond death, or death beyond life?

The question remains a question still,

Through the everlasting metamorphosis

Of the insoluble drill

Of life and death, of truth and untruth,

Of war and peace, and above all,

Of the God in man and the man in God

To sound the clarion call:

"I am the resurrection and the life.

He that exercises faith in me, even though he dies,

Will come to life; and everyone that is living

And exercises faith in me will never die at all."

(Bhowanipore Cemetery)

THE SATISFACTION

If I watch the world through the dreams of mine,

There's nothing to repent

For that's the place where my joy and sorrow

In total calmness blend.

Dreams of darkness, dreams of brightness,

Of devastation, resurrection and all

Seem to weave themselves into one whole unit

In life's great dancing hall.

If I could find the charms and marvels

In my dreamland, why, then why

You won't find your peace and quietness

Which unexplored, in your dreamland lie?

Convert your life then, into a world of dreams

Where nothing more could be

Aspired, craved or ever wished for

On the slightest earthly plea.

Revel in the wonderland

Where wants lie satisfied

Through the elixir of the realisation

That all your wants have died.

STORY OF MY SURVIVAL?

As I wander on the lonely tracts

Of life, being all alone,

Silence plays its divine music

And I rejoice on my own.

My loneliness here finds its voice

And erupts in ecstasy

To find His presence all around

And as far as I could see.

I need no partner in the mortal world,

I need no joy or sorrow;

I wait for none to fill my today

Or my anticipations tomorrow.

Here I bask in freedom's rays

And throw my arms around

The calm and peace which prevail here

Through the universe's silent sound.

Here I find my truest mates

In the passing breeze and flowing streams

And the open skies and floating clouds

And the ever smiling pure sunbeams.

Here then lies my peace retrieved

As I touch the space which floats

Along the contours of my mortal body

With divinity's silent notes.

Here then I'll have found my partner

In the silent environment

To walk alone in peace and pleasure

Through the mortal hours spent

In course of the long and tedious journey

Of life and of existence

And while composing the story

Of my survival hence.

The Quiet Search

I've exhausted myself of my joys

And my sorrows remain to be

Exhausted from my mortal world

Where I've lost my mirth and glee.

Sleepless hours through the night,

Restless hours through the day,

Have kept me engaged in my pursuit

Of a calm and peaceful way.

The massive thrusts of destined strokes

Have pushed me forward all along

The drive where life has seen both God's

And the Devil's agents crowd and throng.

And as soon as I shall rid myself

Of the thoughts which strike the tragic notes,

My soul shall taste its natal freedom

To spin life's finest anecdotes.

Free from all my nocuous glory

And from all my rhythmic pains,

Emancipation is bound to find its way

Through the clearance which, in the midst, remains.

The gusts of wind which blow tonight

Have swept away the fallen leaves

And cleared the passage where my mind

Strolls in peace and quietly weaves

Stories of a life to be

Where neither calm nor thunder

Can play a role to mess with life

And tear it all asunder.

THE TRAVEL

A-ha, A-ha, from the bounded barriers of the earth

My travel has now begun

Towards the boundless hall of eternity

Where I shall enter and shall shun

The mortal chains which had me tied

Firmly to the ground

Where I bled in agony with no one to

Hear my distressed sound.

A-ha, A-ha, my wings are growing

To take off and to lift

The 'anima' to reach the anima mundi'

Where I'll lie in peace adrift.

I've never been more happy than

The hours I am spending here

To prepare for my onward flight

Towards the endless unknown mystic sphere.

More than ever I do now

Love the earth anew

And everything which my eyes now capture

Turns golden in my view.

And the propensity to give my all

To the world below my feet

Ere I leave forever and bid goodbye,

Is a feeling which is sweet

And precious through the days I am

Here with all my friends,

Till darkness on my human eyes

And light on my soul descend.

<u>MY FAILURE</u>

My time rolls by with speeding paces

Faster than my own,

Dragging me through sundry places

Known or yet unknown.

Much before I find the time

To complete the steps I've taken,

I'm further dragged with scars and bruises

Along the path that's God-forsaken.

And all along the carriage-way,

My journey spells out doom

As I fail to welcome the rushing time

With a little bit of room.

THE WINNER

This is where life's road has been

Sharply bifurcated,

Where one is for my human powers

And the other for what's already fated.

I take the one which holds my powers

And find my success scaled

Through sheer dint of my manly efforts

Which hardly ever failed.

I return then to walk along

The other road which lies

Unexplored, where fate has ordained

My destiny below the skies.

There I likewise find myself

Filled with success and

All that's needed to make my life

Splendid, great and grand.

If that be so, the equation is

Same in both the cases,

Where fate seems to win the game

By always drawing the aces.

SONG OF A LAWYER

As I look back through the history of times

And collect the rusted fragments of my life,

I think I've learnt the painful lessons

Of the propensity to live and survive

Along the rough and rugged stressful roads

Which still now lie ahead,

Where my weary feet still bleeds much more

Than they had earlier bled.

Still now I am haunted by

Insecurities' condemned ghosts

Where adversities of sundry orders

Are the most unwanted hosts.

Uncertainty still now plays its role

Of apprehension as to what shall happen tomorrow,

Whether I shall roll and bask in wealth

Or rot in penury and steal, beg or borrow.

No more than ever looms above

The apparition of the thunder

Of unsecured risks of a fatal nature

Which may tear this life asunder.

Every moment passes with

Trembling thoughts as these,

For uncertainties and insecurities in lawyers' lives

Shall never ever cease.

A thankless journey through fog and clouds

Where the tunnel never ends

And life ebbs out through ceaseless work

Till mighty death descends.

The Stand Of The Passing Moments

As I roamed alone in the wilderness,

I heard a voice: "Seek and you shall find

The meaning of these lonesome moments

Superbly defined!"

I halted then and asked each moment:

"Hi there, wait and tell me once

The meanings of your diverse 'mudras'

In course of your cryptic dance,"

And then the passing moments, one by one,

Clarified their stand

Through answers which I quote below

Which are easy to understand:

"One is meant for the charms of nature,

One for the earthly odds,

One for destiny's dictates and

One for the divinity of the Gods.

One for the love of a lovely woman,

One for ceaseless work,

One for the sunshine in the day,

One for the moonlight in the dark.

One for peace and one for friendship,

One for the wisdom of the sages,

One for your conscience, kind and fair,

One for humanity through the ages.

One for loving all around you,

One for thanksgiving,

One for all you have received,

One for life and one for living.

One for expectations and hopes,

One for all that you can presently see,

One for your strides towards perfection,

One for all that's yet to be."

THE DEDICATION

When I dedicate my within and all

To meet your requirements,

Oh, the pleasure! Oh, the treasure!

Oh, the sounds and scents!

Oh, the magic which then flows

And fills my soul at once

To carve a niche for peace amidst

Life's monstrous dance.

In me, the storm soon subsides and

Stillness finds its place

To make some room for the entry of

Your glory and Your grace.

This little space was needed much

To realise and understand

The magnificence and the magnitude

Of the cosmos where You stand.

My entire life will find its meaning

Through every pain and scar

If You could just bless me with

The slightest fraction of what You are!

Enter, Lord, with all Your glamour

Into my existence's vacant hall

Where the place is cleared of all that's earthly

As I have dedicated my within and my all.

OBLIVIOUS

In the melee of a thousand works

You are always around,

Yet I never ever think of You

Despite Your vision and Your sound.

You pass by me but I hardly ever

See You passing by;

You beat Your drums so often yet

My ears are deaf and dry.

Countless times You've shown the road

Where I should place my foot,

But I've availed myself of every chance

To deviate from the route.

Still then at daybreak with folded hands

I pray for what I pine,

Oblivious of all that's already granted

In this existence of mine.

THE HOPE ACROSS

Tragedies which have marred my life

Have equally lent their charms

By pushing me with their whipping canes

Right into Your caring arms.

And that's how I have survived when

My interiors were dry

And I thought that I must bid the world

My tear-filled last goodbye;

It was then that You had come in silence

Unknowingly from behind

To give me back my worth in gold

With a twist of fate by Your mastermind.

And much before the time I could

Feel the final pangs of grief,

Your soothing touch on the scars of life

Ushered in my quiet relief.

In every step I take in life,

In every word I speak,

You have quietly played Your role

Where nothing is ever bleak;

Nothing is without a meaning and

Nothing is without an order;

If despair fills the surroundings now,

There's hope across the border.

THE ASPIRATION

Sometimes in the early morning,

If it rains as it is raining now,

My existence with all its sufferings

Seems to take a unique vow:

To merge myself with nature's romance

And drench my spirit in the rains

And make love with divinity and forget all

The earthly sources of my pains.

This and nothing more than this

Is all that I need to find

In my quest for peace and emancipation

While leaving the entire world behind.

Let me therefore cast asunder

Fate's dictates as they are,

And seek your glory all by myself

Despite tragedy's painful bar.

Give me what I really need,

Don't give me what I don't;

Give me peace and not such gifts

The lack of which I've never mourned.

REFLECTIONS

Sometimes when I aimlessly

Cast my vision far away

At the horizon where the setting sun

Paints the sky with its sinking ray,

And ends the day with its striking colours

Smeared on the clouds around

Where fantasy in all its splendid forms

Lifts me from the ground

To dizzy heights of an absurd order

Which makes me prone to think

Whether the day when my life will end

Should also bear a common link:

Whether the day when I shall also sink

Into the horizon of my existence

Shall be likewise painted with the colours

Erupting from my finest sense?

And whether, when I shall pass away,

I'll see a colourful ending day

Where life and death, like light and darkness

Shall mingle all the way?

AT LAST!

Songs which were never sung before,

Are being sung now with the zeal

Which time has infused in my soul

To confront, face and deal

With the inevitable tryst with the Creator who

Shall stretch His welcome hand

To greet me in His unknown world

And lift me from this land.

Thoughts which never struck before,

Have likewise gained there force

Into the active field of a brooding mind

Waiting to end the course

Of the flow of life with steady motions

To meet the only friend

Who stays incognito throughout life

And reveals Himself at the end.

<u>FRIENDSHIP</u>

The more I sense and feel the motions

Of the passing life around,

And the more I advance through the terrains

To reach my destined ground,

The more the realisation dawns on me

That not I, but also every other man

Is alone and on his own;

And a friend is a misnomer in the circus

Where no friendship could be ever grown.

In a world where survival is the basic theme,

A selfless friend is a myth,

For somewhere there must always be

Some self-interest, even a little bit.

My desire is to love you dearly

And that is precisely where

My interest lies as a friend to you

And offer you my love and care,

Lest I should lose you from my life,

Lest we should have to part:

A friend, am I, if I do not love you

Selflessly from my heart?

And if I ever lose my way, my dear,

Into the devil's dungeons where

I transform myself and set my paces

Through Satan's thoroughfare,

And extend my hand of friendship to

Hold your hands, my dear,

Will you touch me then, will you kiss me then,

Will you, will you, dear?

THE BLISS

Tonight the moonlight has wrapped me with

Its magnificence around

My soul and spirit which have now

In divine ecstasy found

Their quiet and silent inner peace

Where all that's painful, all that's stressful is absorbed

in that light

Leaving me alone to bask thereunder

In angelic delight.

By the magic waves of the golden light

Spread out all around,

A celestial art of the divine kingdom

Finds its earthly ground.

All my unhealed scars and wounds

Are deleted one by one

And yield their place to quiet repose

In course of life's final run.

This is my bliss of existence,

And my charm to survive,

In the moonlight sonata

Of a nightlong life.

THE ONUS

Far away from normal regions,

I must henceforth roam,

For I must somewhere find my peace

And treat it as my home.

A home away from home, is it?

Or is it just a cause

To escape what I failed to find

And did not care to pause?

Or is it just a means to shift

The onus which rests on me

To search for peace not elsewhere but

Within my own entity?

SMILE!

Smile and the entire world around

Will smile with you in turn

In course of which the vibes of smiling

Will, like coastal waves return

To fill the void in the beach of life

Where life has gone amiss,

And seal the rueful tragic spots

With peace and divine bliss.

Smile and you will feel inside

Your own heart and mind

The reciprocations of the universe

Inherently intertwined.

In the strangeness of the mystic magic

Spread through the universe,

Your smiles in life will help to compose

A splendid poetic verse

With which you can view your life

In the garden of the Gods

And discard with the ease of a master

All your mortal odds.

Smile and your graceful profile shall

Help to fill the dearth

Of peace and happiness and of a heaven

On this ever warring earth.

THE DIFFERENCE

Unique are your manifestations

Through Your artwork spread around

Everywhere to quietly relive

My life and to slowly impound

All pains and sufferings from where I find

A refreshed life which glows

With understandings of my soul and spirit

Where all my closed and rusted doors

Are flung open through which I can

So clearly watch and see

The adversities, misfortunes and what not,

Of others, worse, yes, worse than me!

I view Your world with staring eyes,

I hear Your sounds with open ears,

I touch both grief and happiness

As life's broad-based hemispheres.

Your artworks comprise both pains and joy

As garlands worn by all

In the conglomeration of all lives on earth

Through existence's endless hall,

Where I have also stepped in as

A fractioned speck of dust

To spend a fractioned speck of time

On the surface of the crust.

But the difference lies where I can surely

See Your work and hear Your sounds

Blessed by the fortune which

Helps me to take my final rounds.

But what with those who have been thrust

In the infernal abyss of endless pains

Where nothing worth their existence—

Nothing, nothing, nothing remains?

Lift Me There!

Far beyond Your galaxies

Where no man has ever reached,—

Lift me there!

At that realm where war and hatred

Are never preached,—

Let me fare!

Or make this earth a seat of peace

Where nature's bounties can

Inject all that nature wants

Into the heart of every man.

Let the divine touch which blessed our lives

When each of us was born

Be tasted but not wasted ever

As we proceed to adorn

Our existence with hopes and laughter,

Remembering to wipe the tears

Of those less fortunate than ourselves

In course of our living years.

And by creating a heaven on this earth,

The pleasure shall be ours

As we leave our marked footsteps

While crossing the rolling hours.

Let us lend our feelings and hands to all

And open our ears and eyes

And share the grief and pains of others

And with all, sympathize;

The symphony of life shall then be raised

To the highest astral station

Where our souls shall find their final placements

In the grandest constellation.

THE LINK

In these soundless hours of the night

The vibrations slowly rise

Of an entity I've been searching across

The wilderness and the skies.

Somewhere in the ancient ages

Far beyond my mortal brink,

I seem to feel a strange adherence

To an unknown mystic link:

A link to which my soul and spirit

Indebted remain

To have matured through the span of time

With happiness and with pain.

The surrounding darkness brings along

The chance to quietly weave

My thoughts to strike a charming balance

Between my pleasure and my grief.

Here it is then, where all my senses

Merge with a single whole,

And disappear into the magnitude

Of that entity's massive role.

Here I find my worth and meaning

Through boundless time and space

As I diffuse myself with all my ego

And dissolve in Your mighty grace.

THE CONTINUATION

Slowly I can feel your greetings

And your cordial invitations

To celebrate our tryst soon after

I cross the last few stations.

And as I cross these one by one,

I hear the fabulous sound

Of charming melodies spun by you

Hovering all around.

Here while crossing the weary miles,

My existence is sprayed

With colours of the life on earth

So wonderfully laid

And spread out on the path I tread

To enable me to learn

The mystic magic of my soul

In course of my quiet return.

Life tastes sweeter at every bend

Seeking confrontation with the ultimate

As it proceeds on its destined motions

To reach the unknown final date.

And my celebrations have already begun

On a grand and high-pitched scale

On the surface of the earth where my

Dreams and fancies still prevail.

And in course of our aspired rendezvous,

The celebrations shall still then continue

At your homeland in the heavens where

There's nothing special, nothing new.

THE DOUBT

When darkness engulfs all my senses

And hopelessness solely reigns,

And in and around my existence,

Devastation remains;

When I stare at all the passing hours

And draw a complete blank,

When life resigns into a cryptic place

Departing from its active rank;

When clouds gather 'fore my eyes

And stall my forward motions

And destiny whips me and strips me of

All my fine emotions;

When shadows of a ghostly order

Follow the steps I take;

When life and living taken together

Themselves are at stake;

When hopes find way into nothingness

And confidence is lost,

And life, for all its adversities,

Humbly pays the cost;

When the massacre has reached its climax

With the ruination of my all,—

At the end of the session, from afar,

I hear your beckoning call!

Shall this soothe my burning spirit

And retrieve from the ash

All that I have lost forever

And all that has turned to trash?

<u>YET TO BE?</u>

Through the sounds of my heartbeats every moment,

His Godly footsteps sound,

While I feel His divine omnipresence

Engulfing me all around.

Hardly a moment passes by

When I fail to watch His rhymes

Spread out through the immeasurable vastness

Of the endless span of times.

Still now, is it not yet time

To put a complete ban

On war and hatred, strife and bloodshed

Between man and man?

Is it not yet time to feel

His presence in us all

And hear our heartbeats sound together

In humanity's massive hall?

How long shall ethnic and honour killings

Or racial murders act as rules

In a so-called civilization crafted by

A handful of human fools?

How long shall His divine goodness

Simply stand and stare

At the atrocities committed by the devil

Along his infernal thoroughfare?

Let the sounds of our heartbeats echo through

This blasted human mess

And usher in a world of peace

And His supreme Godliness!

THE UNENDING SEARCH

Through the passage of the years, I have

Still not found the road

To relieve me of life's great burden

And the stressful onerous load

Which despondency has thrust on me

And solitude has laid

Where all options to unload the burden

Have been fatally stayed.

Now then that what remains of

Life and existence,

In the context of Your manifestation,

Leaves a meaning and a sense,

Where I can surrender unto You

All that I have missed

In my mortal years, till the day

Ordained for the tryst

With You, after I leave forever

My earthly shape and form

At the end of life and at the end

Of this undue thunderstorm

With darkened hours reigning 'tween

The devil and the divine

To appreciate and take cognizance of

All that is really mine

In terms of sufferings which have led

Me to recognize

You in Your omnipresence

Before my tear-filled human eyes.

The ARRIVAL

Since long I've been striving hard

To search for the painter hiding in

The network of my heart and soul

And see what's painted deep within.

In the heaps of pleasure, I found Him not,

Nor in my happy hours;

I missed Him in the fields of life

Where tasteful success towers.

I lost His tracks when I glided smoothly

Through life's amazing drives;

I felt Him not where otherwise

I felt all happy vibes.

But just as I was about to yield

And to give up all my hopes,

And just when life had pushed me hard

To slide down the destined slopes;

And just when all my painful moments

Gathered one by one,

And just when all my adversities

Had their network spun;

And just when all my tragic hours

Marked my destined times

And just when I was deprived of

Life's happy vibrant rhymes;

And just when all these fatal blows

Silenced all my senses,

The painter surfaced with his paints

By breaking all the fences

And painted all those rueful places

With the colours of the rainbow's arc

To lend the shine and brightness to

The areas which were sad and dark.

And thus the painter came and shall

Stay as long as I

Shall suffer pains and stare in agony

At the distant horizon and the sky.

Questions & Answers

Many a time through my existence

I have asked:

'You have blown life into me

But why can't I

Use it fully?'

You kept silent through your moves

While making the world dance

At your feet,

Till one day you answered

Quite coolly:

'That's because I always wield

The supreme power

Since the ancient birth of man

And the universe,

In entirety;

And I never intend

To allow man to use

His life fully

Lest he should match

Divinity.'

As time rolled by,

I asked again:

'You have blown life into me

But why can't I

Use it fully?'

You asked me to wait

With undue patience

Through stress and storms

Till my life was exhausted

Almost wholly.

And you answered but

You changed your stance

And hurled your answer

When life was about

To depart:

'That's because I intended

To help man reach perfection

Through the feeling and realization

Of incompleteness

And make Divinity his integral part!'

THE TASTE OF SILENCE

Through my brooding hours in the night,

The taste I find is sweet,

Of solitude with all its glory

Ready to coyly greet

My soul and spirit and indeed

My entire existence

Where destiny whips my life to bleed

With a barbecue of its spoilt remains.

I savour the quietness all around

And find my inner place

Within the silent depths of me, myself

With all His divine grace.

And that is where my ecstasy finds

An expression of Your frame,

Where You and I do merge together

And become one and the very same.

The pleasure then is a pleasure always

Embedded deep within

The nucleus of my very being

Studded with piety and with sin.

Thus the sweetness of solitude

Relentlessly multiplies

And colours the darkness of my life

Where my supreme happiness lies.

THE EQUATION

The wonderland here, where all my urges

Amalgamate and form

A massive sense of being with You

Amidst the raging thunderstorm

Of life and all its ramifications

Where nothing, nothing, nothing can

Satisfy my longings ever

As spread out through my mortal span,

Beckons me with all that's charming,

And all that's peaceful, while

A divine aura transforms me,

My spirit and my style.

Here again, life reveals itself

With all its playing cards

And every brush of air which passes,

Speaks a thousand words.

The pull is much too great and mighty

For me to brush aside

The addiction which draw me there

For a quiet and silent glide

Through the halls of dust, from where indeed

I was one day born,

And where I'll return when life shall itself

With death adorn.

THE TRANSFORMATION

'When suffering transforms itself into ecstasy,

When pain transforms itself into joy',**

The mortality within me transforms itself

Into immortality's lover-boy.

And the concussion which jolts my soul

Amidst the clash of wisdom and ignorance,

Makes way to lead me to newer heights

And refine my human existence.

My pain is ignorance, my joy is wisdom

And the interaction between the two,

Is a never-ending process from

Which peace must draw its clue.

Unto pains I'm grateful, unto sufferings, indebted,

For those are the mighty sources

From where You fill my void and vacuum

And strengthen all my living forces.

When more than ever I have a reason to

Shed my tears and weep,

More than ever there's a reason then

To hug You in my sweep

And find my peace and happy hours

Spread out everywhere

Through infinity and the unfathomable

Which within me, themselves seem to bare.

** **Excerpt from The Book of Wisdom. Courtesy: Osho International Foundation**

The Balancing Act

I have a mind which speaks to me

Often like a child;

I have a heart which beats the drums

Of the untamed and the wild.

I have a soul which always seeks

The outer world beyond;

I have a mortal within me

Which seeks the earthly bond.

My happiness seems to weld itself

With gainful pursuits strewn around;

My sorrows seek to tune my strings

To extract the sweetest sounds.

My passions seek to care for those

Whom I love and adore;

My hatred seeks to spurn them out

Who do not fit my score.

My feelings find a wealth of pleasure

In the vicinity of my friends around;

My senses droop with depressed thoughts

Of those who have left the earthly ground.

I have some hopes which seek to build

Castles in the air;

Likewise I have aspirations

Which end in sheer despair.

I have my wisdom as my guide

To lead me through the times;

I have my follies to push me back

Into the world of sickly grimes.

I have a human being in me

Which seeks to oust the devil's charge;

Yet I have a room where the devil creeps

To wreck and oust my human urge.

And throughout my life I've tried to strike

A balance between the two,

But in spite of all my finest efforts,

I've hardly found a clue.

RENAISSANCE

I'll explore the outer self beyond

With my mortal visions here

And implore divinity to descend

Within the depths of my interior.

The blasts of wind shall slash my life,

The waves shall lash my crease,

And in the chaos and discord of my life,

Through these, I'll find my peace.

And so on and so forth, through the thunderstorms

Generated through destiny and executed by fate,

I'll find the charms of life and living

Before I meet and merge with the Ultimate.

Not a word of grief and agony

Shall I ever spread,

Not a tear through the weeping eyes

Shall I ever shed;

But I shall store these painful moments

In the closets of my heart

And extract the strength and power from

Tragedies' classic art.

From the debris of my shattered dreams

I'll build a huge empire

In the core of which shall be always lit

Grief's eternal fire.

Priorities Ignored

Fortuitous? Or is it so?

A question which always hounds

On the rippled surface of my mind

Where Your artistry surrounds

My life and the entire universe

With the touch of Your magic wand

While we do not ever ascertain

What we want or do not want.

And as I fight over petty things in life,

I hardly am aware,

How the universe is fine-tuned to

A perfect balance everywhere.

And if man could have wielded

A fractioned fraction of Your powers

And used it with due love and passion

Through his numbered living hours,

The sunshine would have seemed then brighter

And the world more colourful than

What they seemed to be before

Such transformation of man.

Is it just by chance that You

Have lent Your art and grace

To all Your motions far and near

Which fall in the perfect place?

Your wizardry has indeed woven

The cult of a rich empire

Only to be set ablaze by man

By igniting an endless fire

Of wrath and war and lust and greed

Without setting forth

The priorities of our aspirations

Within our playing court.

THE DRUMBEATS

And with my heartbeats, the drums of life

Also go on beating,

As the moments pass by, one by one,

Slowly deleting

The miles remaining to be crossed

Till I reach the unknown mystic end

Where divinity in its astral forms

Must descend;

Where all my questions yet unanswered

Shall find their answers shaped,

And the soul shall find its realizations

Which so long had escaped;

Where urges of the flesh and blood

Shall lose their sensuous meaning

In an ambience where the spirit shall

Find a better leaning;

Where life shall find its lessons learnt

To welcome death with grace

And the footsteps left on the earth behind

Shall mark their finest trace;

Where no pain shall be strong enough

To make me weep and grieve,—

No joy can be overwhelming

To build a world of make-believe;

Where the magnitude of the universe

Shall find its room in me

And over-flood the seams of life

In course of the merging spree;

Where my existence and that of Yours

Shall be promiscuous with ease

And I'll be driven home at last

Through my endless search for peace.

LESSONS

Through whatever angle you view your life,

There are lessons to take—

Just don't close your eyes, just don't sleep,

But keep yourself sensitively awake.

Whether it is through your finest joys

Or dreariest tragedies,

Take a lesson, learn a lesson,

Make an issue out of these.

Learn to make the platform of your life

Solid through your sorrows;

And through your joys and happiness,

Paint your todays and tomorrows.

When the nights are dark and the wind is still,

Learn to quietly concentrate;

When the day is sunlit and your life is active,

Learn to thank your God and fate.

When you breathe so fully with other creatures

The same God-gifted air,

And drink the same water of the earth,—

Take a lesson and learn to share.

When you see the trees shed all their leaves

And drape themselves anew,

Shed your grief and wear your hopes—

And take a lesson from that view.

When you see the raindrops cool the earth

As they relentlessly fall,

Learn to cool the burning earth

By pouring peace for all.

Take a lesson from all creatures,

Find out what they do,

Take a lesson from their movements—

Learn your lessons from them too.

Lessons are scattered everywhere,

It's for you to find and learn;

It's for you to 'stoop to conquer' them

At every strategic turn.

Take your lessons, learn your lessons

And enrich yourself as a man

To participate with joy and pleasure

In God's and nature's great game-plan.

The Recreation

Restless mind, Oh, restless mind!

Let me stop and pause

To heal the spirit's ailments and

Obliterate the cause.

Here then do I stop and pause

To see the rising morning sun

Paint the sky with diverse colours

When the day has just begun;

Here then do I stop and pause

To see the cloud-flakes floating by,

To reach and touch the mountain peaks

And to return as showers from the sky;

Here then do I stop and pause

To watch the motions of the life

Bubbling around my existence

With the urge to create and survive;

Here then do I stop and pause

To marvel at Your artistry

Spread through Your massive universe

And indeed, within every man and me;

Here then do I stop and pause

To find Your shapes concealed

In every striking act of Yours

With which my life is fatally sealed;

Here then do I stop and pause

And try to peep into my own within

And face and confront the restless thoughts

Which ceaselessly dance and spin;

Here then do I stop and pause

To seek my own defaults

And cause a frantic search to find

A scrap of gold in my spirit's vaults;

Here then do I stop and pause

To understand that I

Am alone, yet omnipotent,

In the bordered realm where I lie;

Let therefore life percolate through the filters

Of reconstruction and review,

And all disorders shall stand amended

To recreate and cherish our lives anew!

The Picture of Existence

When I lend my years to the sounds of silence,

The sounds of divinity call,

And absorb within its massive sphere,

My grief and happiness and my all.

And the icons of my joy and sorrow

Sculpted in my life

Find wider horizons and newer meanings

In the quest of an overdrive.

My happiness thus finds its placement

To fill up all that's void

And merge with all that's celestial

While my soul lies overjoyed.

And my grief shall blossom into a flower,

The fruits whereof shall be

Creations out of the pains of life

Spread out within me.

And the two shall find their fulfillment

As they tend to merge and draw

A bizarre picture of my existence

Where Your Godhead casts its awe!

CONFUSIONS

I never know what pains me always

And I never understand

What should be my route to peace

And what should be my stand.

My heart weighs heavy with a load

As I wearily travel down the lanes

Of memories lost in oblivion

Smeared with shimmering pains.

Touch them I can't, see them I can't,

But I can just about sense

The shades of events lost for ever

In clouds quite deep and dense.

My entire system strains and struggles

But fails to solve and analyse

These unknown spasms of such pains

Which like smoking embers rise

And choke my being and existence

Where I can't freely breathe

But roam with an outward show of joy

With painful currents underneath.

And I watch the world around

Where laughter and tears, joy and grief

Travel hand in hand;

Where a new leaf

Of life is turned

Through passing time

Striking a natural balance

Between discord and rhyme—

Where the discord means me

And the rhyme means You—

An art par excellence

With a complete view.

The Rainbow-Chaser

Life must sometimes fill its vacuum

With futile aspirations

Of a rainbow-chaser whose fancied colours

Paint all passing stations.

That's the time when lurid thoughts

Turn into sublime hopes—

The raison d'etre of living a life

By negotiating the fatal slopes.

As destiny holds my life to ransom,

I gain my escape through

The pleasures created on my own

Where I find the hidden clue

To solve the crossword of this ruckus

Called life and existence

Which tend to pull my soul apart

And mock my humane sense.

A man must sometimes ransack life

To find a slice of time

Which he can call his very own

And unite with his spirit's rhyme

Where no one else but he alone

Shall triumph in solitude;

Where no one else shall have the right

To interfere or intrude;

Where his loneliness shall fetch his laurels

For bridging the heaven and the earth

By converting his void into happiness

And feel and bask in his negative worth.

Destiny's dreams shall then be fulfilled

And so shall man's

With matching success to materialize

Divinity's unknown plans.

A Different Me

Now here in the somber stillness in the air

I breathe the cosmic waves,

To search for the different me in me

Where the inner spirit craves

The touch of peace, the feel of content

At which I clutch to live

Like a drowning man at a floating straw

Where there's nothing to retrieve

In the massive span of endless time

From where I've borrowed a tiny part

To make my presence felt on earth

Till the final day when I'll depart.

And through the tiny span of borrowed time

I must live and smile

And balance all my tragic hours

With those of a happy style.

I must absorb the charms and colours

Spread out everywhere

And spurn my grief to churn itself

To find its joyous share

From the wealth that's strewn in abundance

In the tiny span of time—

The time between my birth and death

Where my inner conflicts rhyme.

And that's where I can recline quietly

Within a different me of sorts

Lodged within my inner me

With the best of life's resorts.

The Lifestyle

Somewhere in my life I need

A precious moment of my own

Where I can enjoy all by myself

And all by myself I can mourn.

Where I can myself feel my life

And all by myself, think of death,

And all by myself treat myself

As the finest friend I ever met.

And that is how through every hour,

My spirit lives to gain

Its priceless link in your universe's

Massive mystic chain.

Unfathomed lies then the pleasure which

Fills my emptiness

And heals my sores which grew like cancer

Through life's distress.

My straying thoughts are composed then

With a fresh and balanced hue

Where all my works lie dedicated

To You and only You.

Nothing ever hurts me then,

Nothing ever pains,

Whether through the warmth of sunlight

Or the wetness of the rains.

Let me live my life in glory

All by myself and all alone,

Shorn of all my futile cravings

Imaged through an earthly zone.

The Sound of Tears

From nooks and corners, least expected,

Life is meant to bear

Sudden pains of great dimensions

Which tend to wreck and tear

The heart to pieces; yet the mind

Must face the world without

Showing even a tinge of sadness

Or speaking your feelings aloud.

What then should the ratio be

Between a smile and suppressed pains?

It's the belief in the God above—

The only option which remains!

The only option through which I seek

The solace and comfort of the soul;

And the solitary avenue through which I walk

Alone to reach life's final goal.

Somehow I must thrust these pains

Into oblivion's dark trash-trays,

And delete the grieving files forever

So that in course of the future days,

Grief shall not hold my life to ransom

And take its painful toll

By flooding the mind all over again

Like waves which twist and roll

Rushing madly towards the landed shores

And fall crashing on the beach

Of the mystic soul, seeking to find

Its creator within its reach.

And while the pains would lie absorbed

In the calm and quietness within me,

I shall merge in complete fusion

With eternity.

INTERPRETATIONS

The World.
A fashion parade of human lives
Of various shapes and forms
With the background filled with disco lights
Camera clicks and thunderstorms.

The Spectators.
In search of the finest contours
Running through ravishing curves
Spelt out by the participants
Catwalking with unspoken verves.

The Rulers.
Decked with the wisdom of the mind
And going by the laws and rules
Pretending to cover their ignorance
By treating the innocent as simple fools.

The Wanderer.
Passing by in a casual mood
And casting a weary glance or two,
Feels tired but sees the ongoing circus,
And wonders, yet fails to find a clue.

The children.
Let loose by the parents on the streets,
Ramble, play and shout,
But never bother to ever unravel
What the mystery is all about.

People.
Teeming millions. Searching for money
And pursuing the rat-race game,
While some others pursue a lifeless life
And a handful pursue fame.

Lovers.
In eternal search for the meaning of love,
Find nothing really ever rests
On love. And satisfaction and peace
Play will-o'-the-wisp defying endless quests.

The Insane.
The children of the kindly God, the finest souls,
For they do not ever comprehend
The intricacies of life and death, of pains and hatred,
And expect nothing and have nothing to repent.

Man.
A fractioned speck in the cosmic space
With a time-bound, star-bound fate,
Forks out precious time for wars and battles,
And to murder, cheat and hate.

Peace.
A forgotten word. An obscure term.
A vanished notion. And all efforts that
Are spent to search for its whereabouts
Are spoilt by the fire and venom spat
BY A BEAUTIFUL DRAGON CALLED MAN.

RATIOS

Half my life is spent by dreaming

Of a life which could have been;

The rest half is simply the confrontation

With the reality in between.

Through the passing fits of pains and laughter

In the worldly rigmarole,

My outward show is not the language

Spoken by my soul.

I have words and questions which

I've preserved in my vault

Where the rightful answers haven't yet

Been installed.

And on days as these when the sun is shaded

And the sky is overcast,

Thoughts like these come rushing in

With a sudden onward blast,

And softly mould my mind to feel

The difference lying between

My dreams which can be dreamt of only

And the reality which can be really seen.

And soon the language of my soul

Shall be the same as of my outward show

Where reality shall rule my existence

And dreams shall be shown the door!

And that's the point where a chapter shall

End and begin

With another question for a future answer:

"Shall I lose or shall I win?"

The Load—Factor

At times this workload haunts me like

An apparition of the dead

Where a million thoughts of a ghoulish order

Follow me in bed.

They cluster around my soul and being

And seek to strangle me

And block all escape routes to freedom

By stealing the master—key.

Soon my mind shall lose its balance

And life shall lose its gait

When I shall have to submit to

The vagaries of my fate.

And time, with the motions of its own

Shall whip my feelings and

Churn them just as the lashing waves

Churn the coastal sands;

For nothing shall revive a fraction even

Of the fondest times behind

To, just for a moment, fetch in part,

The long-lost peace I've left behind.

The Supreme

Destiny is always the royal ruler

Where life is just a tool,

And it's not for you or me to alter

The charted ordained rule.

And everywhere this axiom is

So very true indeed

For if the destined mandate is to bleed,

Then bleed we must, we'll have to bleed.

No measure of hope, no amount of aspiration

Can ever pave our mortal way

For destiny being the monarch of our lives,

Inevitably has the final word and say.

And as mute spectators we must simply stand

And surrender to the whims

Of destined dictates from an unknown world

Just as the dictator deems.

And in between we shall wear out ourselves

With unspent passions and

Some day end our mortal existence

Like castles on the sand.

The Walk

This is a lane where I have walked

Many a saddening time

And I hear today the long lost hours

Nostalgically chime

And create ripples in my blood as if

The history is revived

Of a tear-filled past which so long had

Unsuccessfully strived

To reveal itself with all its nuances

Which merge now with the present's stream

Where my tears, in the confluence of the wonders

Of the past and the present, gleam.

And as I walk along this lane, I feel

My memories find their clues

To reopen all that's lost and forgotten

And thrust into the blues.

Here then emotions from my deep within

Surface on the heights

Where the spirit's passions on a finer land

Find the Godly lights.

And that's the place where the soul of mine

Finds refinement and peace

While traveling alone in the silence of

Quiet lanes as these.

<u>Seaward ho!</u>

On the ever—swinging trapeze of human life

We stand and shape our daily art

'midst light and darkness, wealth and poverty,

Joy and sorrow, as ordained by our fatal chart.

And under the 'big top' of the endless sky,

The circus goes on and on;

And every passing moment shortens life

Till a death is born.

Or till our realization ripens

Into maturity and brings forth

An amalgamation with the cosmic realm

As the final halting port—

The final harbour to unload all

The burden of our joy and sorrow

And relieve ourselves of the undue weight

Of mortal passions while going out to the sea tomorrow.

Seaward ho! Seaward ho! Join me if you wish;

For here I go! Here I go!—To seek my peace and bliss!

And I shall not return, nor shall you

If you accompany me and say 'adieu'

To the world we leave behind. And we

Shall merge ourselves in oneness with

The cosmic sea.

The Journey From Within

My chest feels heavy with unseen burdens,

With unknown reasons, my heart feels sore,

As I face the heavy blasts of winds

Which dash against my chamber door.

It's midnight now, but the night is restless

As much as my soul now is,

While groping vainly for answers to

Life's ever endless quiz.

Nothing really keeps me quiet,

Nothing really satisfies

My longings just to find some peace

In a world where only quietness lies.

And as I try to rise and build my dreams

And invite You to lend a hand,

My entire effort is blown away

Like a brittle castle on the sand.

Must a second's turn of unseen events

Rip apart my stand?

Must the charms of life shoot out of reach

Before I could understand?

Yet the radiance of existence

Casts its vibrant spell

Unsheathing all that's low and dormant

From their cold and covered shell.

And the impulse gains its unspent motions

And raises the traveller in my genes

Where life with all its doubts and firmness

Reflects what it really means.

And throughout the rough and rugged terrains,

As I accelerate and drive,—

The 'aurora borealis' of an uncertain fate

Shimmers along my life.

The Entry of Magnificence

It's nice to let these hours pass

With their own slow and lingering gait;

And it's pleasing to my earthly senses

Just to watch and wait:

To watch the ongoing arts and crafts

And the handiworks with which

Nature dresses or undresses

On its massive endless pitch;

To watch the motions or the stillness

Which fill the vacuum space

Of passing time with charms and magic

Through every moving phase;

To watch the sunrays spray their colours

On the canvas of the earth,

And help me create in my soul

An amazing wonder-art.

AND then to wait,—and wait I must,—

To absorb and feel in me

The rhythms of the universe

And the vibes of infinity;

To wait for all that I have been

Longing all along

To open all my senses to

Hear life's resonant song;

To wait for just that single moment

Which fills the entire human mind

Where divinity quietly steps inside

And the universe slowly trails behind.

A Dreamer's Pleasure

If God would have ever walked on earth

Attired as a man,

War would have proclaimed war on itself

And ordered its complete ban.

But then these are useless thoughts

As man shall never behave

Till times hereafter when the ghost of God

Shall rise like a monster from its grave

And overpower all wrongs and sins

With an awful demonic drive

And allow the innocent and the honest

To peacefully live and thrive.

Let man therefore wait and see

A walking God with a demon's clout

Where life should be a dreamer's pleasure

And peaceful living is all about.

The Walk of Life

My search for peace goes on and on

With a frantic urge to find

A place where all my restless thoughts

In You shall lie resigned.

And in course of all this chaos and discord

In my mortal roundabout,

My senses surface on the crust of life

As I feel my time is running out.

Yet at times when passing hours bring

Sudden moments to rejoice,

I hear at the backstage of my life

Your resonant voice.

Likewise when those moments of

Grief and sorrow intervene,

Your voice resounds once again

Through my heartbeats deep within.

And I should realize through the span of time

Which is still now left for me,

That my home of peace through joy and grief

Lies in Your proximity.

And by the time I'll end my walk

And leave behind my warring thoughts,

I shall no more need this world

In the peaceful abode of the Gods.

Simply Nothing

I've shoved my life to absurd limits

Through sleepless nights like these

Where nothing seems to fill the slots

And cure this strange disease.

Nothing seems to find an answer

To all these absurd thoughts

And nothing seems to smoothly join

The oddly spread out dots.

Nothing seems to weave a pattern

Of a dreamland 'round my life,

Nothing seems to deftly balance

The weird and reckless drive.

Nothing seems to calm my senses

And find a place to rest,

Nothing seems to break the shackles

And bring out my very best.

Nothing seems to live in me

And nothing seems to die;

Nothing seems to stand 'fore me,

And nothing seems to lie.

Nothing seems to blossom here,

Nothing seems to wither even,

And nothing seems to straighten out

All that's rough and quite uneven.

Nothing seems to convince me

Why I should live and smile;

And nothing seems to convince me

Why I should die and be sterile.

The Equilibrium

God and Satan, turn by turn,

Play truants in my soul,

And as I rush to greet the one, the other

Takes its fatal toll.

The waves of success and of ruins

Cast their awful forms

Raising sandstorms when life is dry

And in happiness, thunderstorms.

Trust I can't, nor confide

In either of the two,

As I cannot ever distinguish

Who is really who.

And that's the reason why I have

Given both the space

To dwell in me with all their bounties

Which reflect on my face.

And if you ever strain yourself

To read my facial links

To find out whether I am holy

Or whether my background stinks,—

Do not ever try to compare

The difference 'tween you and me,

'Cause you and I are human beings

On the endless unknown sea.

And that is where I have my ties

With both the evil and the good

And that is where I firmly stand

Where man since the birth of man had stood!

I Exist!

Henceforth I shall extract the best

Of the best out of me

And likewise extract the worst

Of the worst as well, in its entirety.

I'll make a mixture of the two

And push it through my blood and veins

And thereby bind the Lord of Lords

In the framework of my mortal reins.

I shall thereby taste the stuff

Of which the entire universe is made

With the essence of the infernal and the divine

To be able to call a spade a spade.

In the fulfillment of life where both

God and the Devil reside,

I'll complete my understanding of the soul

Side by side.

My qualities shall be draped outside

Both in black and white,

While I shall be a perfect man

Within myself right inside.

I shall draw in me the pleasures of

Both darkness and of light

And let my spirit blossom into

Existence's grand delight!

Ode to Solitude

In the vicinity of my heart and mind,

Heaps of solitude lie;

I pick them up now one by one

And hurl them at the sky—

Do you hear their silent sounds

While you are passing by?

Raise your ears and lift your eyelids

As you feel the passing breeze,

And hear the whispers planted therein

And the murmur of the trees—

Haven't you ever heard my solitude

Speaking all through these?

Refine all your human senses,

Explore all your roaming lanes,

Unleash all your trekking spree

Through mountain heights and desert plains—

Did you never feel my friend,

That's where my solitude quietly reigns?

Once upon a time long back,

I had lots to smile,

Unlike the way you see me now

On life's lonely isle.

Can't you sense my solitude

With its impeccable grand profile?

Evensongs in my soul and spirit,

Exaltations in my tired nerves,

Flashbacks within my mental screens,

Ecstasies within my mortal verves!

Solitude, ah, solitude!

My ode to thy strange reserves!

<u>Nothing Special</u>

There's nothing special about the millennium.
There's nothing special about 1.1.2000.

It's just another day—
When the sun shall rise,
The birds shall sing,
The wind shall blow
And church-bells ring.

It's just another day—
When the sun shall set
And the moon shall gleam
And the night shall fall
And man shall dream.

It's just another day—
When the child shall play
And man shall toil,
The wife shall cook
On the earthly soil.

It's just another day—
When time shall pass
And man be born
And shall die
From night to morn.

It's just another day—
When thirst and hunger
Shall make millions cry,
Where half the world's a stage
And the other half's a sty.

It's just another day—
Where contrast plays
The everlasting game
With poverty and obscurity
Matched with wealth and fame.

It's just another day—
When man shall think of peace
But practise not;
And practise war
Without a thought.

It's just another day—
When all my wounds and pains
Shall raise their Stygian heads
And make me lie and bleed
On their thorny beds.

It's just another day—
When man shall rejoice
Over a wrong notion of time
Which hasn't begun and doesn't end
With the wall-clock's chime.

It's just another day—
When I shall search as always
In vain for Thee
In the vast wilderness
Of eternity.

It's just another day—
So common for me
When I can embrace you and say
'I love you darling!'
In my own special way.
Oh! It's just another day!

1st. January, 2000.

The via-media

These painful spasms are my balms

Which bring forth the understanding

Of life with all its subtle meanings,

Its existence and standing.

That's the point where divinity shall

Soothe my sufferings while

All the tragedies in my life

Should find a cause to smile.

That is where my life's Hedonics

Finds its inherent charms

On the gymkhana where pain and pleasure

The superiority of each affirms.

Without one the other shall

Inevitably face its great defeat,

Just as a man without a woman must

Be ever incomplete.

And with tragedy ruling a part of life

And comedy, the other part,

A balance seems to be struck between

A science and an art—

A science, where the loss is measured

In concrete terms,—

An art, where from the ruins of losses,

Resurrection extends its welcome arms!

<u>REDESCRIBING MYSELF</u>

Sometimes the intensity of my pains

Is music to my ears,

Nay, music to my soul

For it soothes my interiors

With the understanding of what you are

To wipe out the parablepsis that life

Should always be filled with happiness

Throughout its onward drive.

And somewhere in the regions where

My pains have so long dwelt,

Somehow you have forced your entry

And made your presence felt.

And just at the mystic juncture where

Our lambent spirits glide

And divinity and the earthly merge

And lose their ranks in pride,

My pleasures rise to envious heights

And throw aside my pains

To absorb all that's ultramundane

In my life's rough terrains.

And the trapeze on which the gymnastics

Of life is performed

And the parameter of survival

Is painstakingly formed,

Finally I find in awe,

My sudden hold

Redescribing my existence

A thousand-fold.

Parting Pains

Do you know my bleeding point?

The bleeding point where I,

In spite of all my virile manhood,

Have to quietly cry?

That's the point of parting when

We have to bid goodbye;

That's the point when I must heave

A painful parting sigh.

That's the point where time does not

Wait to indulge love,

That's the point where you must fly

Away like a parting dove.

That's the point when I aspire

To hold you fastened tight,

That's the point where you must darling

Vanish perforce from my sight.

That's the point where all my cravings,

Passions and urges fail

To hold you back with pleading arms

And many a tear and wail.

That's the point where intense love

Begets intense scorn,

That's the point where pressing demands

Of genuine love are born.

That's the point where you must darling,

Ignore my bleeding spot,

For priorities greater than our love

Are destined to be brought.

That's the point where you must darling,

Break away from me

And let me bleed, and bleed alone,

While you'll be rendered free

From my captivating embrace which

Is a burden on your wings

And a torture on your flowered structure

Where holding simply irks and stings.

My bleeding spot shall ooze out blood

Every parting moment, while

You shall bid me farewell, darling,

With your parting kiss and smile.

Statement of Facts

In my soul,
Your image reigns.
Your touches travel
Through my veins.
In my heart,
Your rhythms beat.
In my spirit,
You have a seat.
In my thoughts,
You are crowd.
In my mind,
You speak aloud.
In my wants,
You do give.
In my life,
You do live.
In my work,
You support.
In my weakness,
You're the fort.
In my pains,
You're my balm.
In my anger,
You're my calm.

You're my solace
In my tears.
You're my music
In my ears.
In the darkness,
You're my light.
You're my wayfinder
In the night.

You're the wave
On which I sway.
You're my company
Everyday.
You're my anchor
In the sea.
In solving problems,
You're my key.
You are there
When I call.
In my 'I',
You are all.
In my being,
You never cease.
In my death,
You'll be my peace.

A CORPSE SINGS NEWTON'S LAW OF GRAVITY

I had lifted myself high in life

And risen to bizarre heights where pride

And luxury found their uncanny home

From where I could not spot the earth

Where I was born and nurtured;

It was not pain then, but sublime joy

That engulfed me as I soaked myself

In my ego that I was above the common;

And basked myself in the complex of superiority

As I wasn't touched by that which was down-to-earth.

Alas! Now I shall have to be lifted by my fellows

From the dusty earth where I have fallen

And be interred in the earth which I had abhorred.

Here unto dust I must return and face the unmasked fact

That the distance with the earth is now no more.

Ah! The pleasure now to feel and embrace

Every speck of dust where I lie

Is mine. For whatever rises up must fall;

And yes, indeed! I have fallen and Newton's

Law of Gravity stands blissfully proved et al.

ADORATION

This is the time when the haloes of

A living Venus shine

And extract the mortal from my soul

And transform it into divine.

And this is where my human senses

Rally around your form

And calm and cool down instantly

My life's thunderstorm.

My glances on your beauty spots

Where God has carved His art

Wrench out all my ecstasies

From the vessels of my heart.

Traumatized, I gaze at you

Where my eyelids hardly blink—

And lip to lip and eye to eye,

I feel the divine link.

When I touch you, I am ushered in

A world of love and trance

Where no one else but you and I

Are the partners in the dance.

The dance of joy, the dance of peace,

And the dance of unison

Where our identity is firmly compressed

Into a complete whole and one.

Here I have the freedom to

Love and hold you in my hands

Where the omnipresent God alone

As the sole and silent witness stands.

Here you stand with all your beauty

Bared and unrobed 'fore my eyes

As if a Venus cast in flesh and blood

Through your undressed shape should crystallize.

And as you breathe, your heaving breasts

With their undulated curve,—

The finest impression of the finest artist

And the finest poet deserve.

Wondergirl, my wondergirl!

I just can't turn my mind and sight

Away from your glamour in the day

And your thoughts throughout the night.

For these are visions where loveliness

In celestial grandeur gleams,

Where I feel and adore the contours of

The woman of my dreams.

Still Unfinished

I am now reaching my journey's end

Where the rainbow bends

And stoops to touch the crust of earth

Where life's horizon ends.

I have lost the hopes to cross

Beyond the ending line

And retain all my liveliness

To search for what's divine.

Sleep I must, yet sleep I'll not,

For the garland that I weave for you

Is still unfinished and still not tied

To hold it in your view.

Grant me strength then, grant me power

To complete all I can

Through the short-lived span of a tired life

And make me a complete man

Before the fire feeds on me

And my bones and body burn

That I may not lose while dying, Lord,

All that I in life should earn.

A Journey to the Past

The fragrance of the flowers and
The scent of incense hold
And lift me lightly like a spectre
Leading me through the days of old.
And the past, with all its glorious colours
Which had faded through the times,
And lost perhaps, its wondrous charms,
Its melodies and its rhymes,
Is resurrected with its class and beauty
And holds me hypnotized
To feel a world I've left behind
And long back solemnized.
Here again now blows in silence
The breeze from the southern seas
Which hovers around my soul and body
Beckoning me with its curious pleas
To step into its unseen chariot
Shaped by the fragrance in the air
And the aroma of the incense sticks
With all their magic flair,

That my mind and spirit may be thrust

To meet again the golden past;

As the present, however sweet and lovely,

Shall never ever last.

For the present shall but always merge

In the annals of the past

As life sails forward like a ship

Where backlashed waves are cast.

Lift me now then lift me Oh!

On the incense of the flowers

And the scent of the incense sticks which lead

To resurrect in glory the forgotten hours.

A LOVESONG FOR YOU

Let the world know in the days to come

That I have loved you as my own;

And within and outside the periphery of my life,

Your affection's stream had flown.

This and nothing more, is my cherished prize

To wet the desert sands,

And fill with flowers blushing through

Life's barren lands.

This and nothing more, scents the air

I breathe, with the fragrance of the Gods

And pours the nectar of the heavens

Into life's empty slots.

This and nothing more, has glorified

The living moments which I spend

To cross the span of allotted time

Through the happiness you have lent.

This and nothing more, is the charming song

Reverberating through my cells

Where your image exists spontaneously

And everlastingly dwells.

This and nothing more, is the unseen base

Where I live and thrive;

And engulfed in your thoughts, I keep myself

Beautifully alive.

A QUESTION

Let me drink Your water, Lord,

And breathe Your air on earth;

Let me see the rays of sun

And feel my mortal worth.

Let me rave like a madman, Lord,

In the marvels of Thy art

And let me fill my heart with charms

Before I depart.

For some day You will come down, Lord,

And take me by Your hand

When I shall have to bid farewell

To all on this mortal land.

Let me sense all pleasures then,

Allotted to me by fate,

As the parting bells seem ringing and

There's not much time to wait.

I wait for the time when You will, Lord,

Invite me and send

Your executor to lead me on

And greet me with my end.

And when I'll meet You, I shall thank

All those down on earth

Who made my life so pleasing since

The first day of my birth.

But I shall also question You

And ask for an apt reply—

As to why should I have had been born

And why should I have had to die?

A Second Home

Here I find my feelings shared

By everyone and all;

Here I have thus myself dared

To bare my heart and fall

Back upon my friends to raise

My confidence and hopes

And help me just to lift myself

From fortune's downward slopes.

Here again I gain the strength

To open wide my wings

And rise above all earthly sorrows

And destiny's piercing stings.

Here, as ever, lies uncovered

Heaven's treasure-chest

With peace and content stuffed therein

And decked with the worldly best.

And the melancholy which engulfs me

With its cloak of sheer despair,

Now transforms itself with its songs

Of happiness in the air.

The fraternity which extends here

Since three decades and more,

Welcomes me at every turn

And offers me its store.

The corridors here through which I tread

And the archways through which I roam,

Fill my mind with the graceful image

Of a living, loving home.

And home this is truly and indeed,

For here I return to bask

In the sunshine and warmth of those

Who think that it's their noble task

To sympathize with the cause of mine

And to beautifully share

The emotions, passions and the feelings

Of a broken pair.

A SONG OF QUESTIONS

I've strived to travel through my thoughts

Fathomless as they are,

And to understand why You and I

Are not at par:

Why should Your Godhead not dwell in me,

And why should not my pains

Dwell in Your Godhead till our status

Equal bearing gains?

Why should I be made to suffer

In silence for your faults?

Why should You not feel the agonies

Born through my defaults?

Why should my life be penalized

Without a reason standing by?

Why You should roam in Your royal style,

And uncensored, unchallenged, lie?

Why should destiny hold my hands

And drag me through these gruesome tracts

While she never asks You for Your hands

To ruin Your life and acts?

Why should You stand untouched by

Feelings which touch me most?

And discard Your promiscuity in the world of man

Where You refuse to play the host?

Why must divinity drift so far

From mankind's lesser ranks

And shy away from answering questions

By leaving the unfilled blanks?

Still I'm crying, still I'm trying

To find answers with my tear-filled eyes

To questions as to why we can't just ourselves,

In disaster, bond and equalize?

A VISIONARY'S PRAYER

Wrap my soul with the wealth of Gods,

Fill my void with glory;

Make my spirit shine like gold,

Cast my life like a fairy story.

Ensure with Your divine goodness

That I may be rich within,

And enrich myself through my prayers

By washing away the soot of sin.

Let my existence on earth

Sparkle like the finest jewels

Won by the Goddesses of the heavens

Or set in the anklets of the dancing belles.

Grant me the stability stored inside

The casket which You hold,

And the confidence to lead my life

And the vision to behold

Your image in every work of mine

And in every move I make

So that the richness of my life and being

Will never be at stake.

Your wealth shall then be the wealth of mine,

And what more should I then need

To rise above the earthly level

With my glittering and enriched mortal breed?

THE ABSTRACT

Roaming with an endless goal

To captivate the mood,

Here I wander all alone

To think of what I should.

And what I should but think except

The mood of affections

Which bind us with their tightened knots

In each and every sense.

Here then I must feel again

The pleasures you had lent

And relive again, though all by myself,

The hours we had spent.

Here then must my imagination

Carve out on its own,

Your shapely figure in the winds

And make it float airborne.

And now with all my mortal urges

To feel and have you by my side,

Your shape resurrects itself from the lifeless

And we stand unified,—

Just as we have stood in life

And just as we will stand,

Forever and forever, even when

We may not hold our hand.

Your shape now rises from the space

And enters in my soul

To make us merge with one another

And to make us a complete whole.

THE ACCESS

When I am alone in the darkness of the world

With silence wrapped around,

I hear Thy beckoning voice, O Lord,

I hear Thy footsteps sound.

And this is where I more than ever

Taste the bliss of life,

So different from the earthly lust

Merely to survive.

For here I find my nest and home

To rest my soul and heart

And reckon in my loneliness

That everywhere Thou art!

No one here is a friend of mine,

No one is my foe,

But I am a friend to everyone

Standing in Thy glow.

And this is the cognizance, O Lord,

Which shapes itself in me,

When all alone in the world of darkness,

I lovingly embrace Thee.

And this is all I have to know

And all I have to learn

To seek an entry in Thy kingdom

Where someday I must return.

THE ADVENTURE

Standing at life's bizarre crossroads

Of endeavour and disorders,

I seek to identify both of these

By brightly painting all the borders

So that I may not lose my course

Through whichever way my fate

Should whip me hard to run along

Zigzag paths or straight.

The path of endeavour is now

The path where I am hurled

To travel, explore and to find

The end of an unknown world.

And as I sweat and reach the end,

I find to my dismay,

I've reached the path of disorders where

I must again begin the day.

Thus then I am set to set

My foot on the other path

Where disorder rules and chaos reigns

Irrespective of the aftermath.

And as I reach the end, I find

To my sheer surprise,

That I have reached the path again

Where my endeavour steadily lies.

And thus is the cycle in course of which

My endeavour stays alive

Through the thrilling adventure of disorders

And chaos which seem to rule my life.

THE AGONY

I am tired of this mind of mine
With brooding thoughts galore,
Meaningless in pith and substance
And burdensome to store.
They multiply like breeding cancer
And suffocate my pleasures, while
I stand aghast in helplessness
With a counterfeited smile.
Must these thoughts be everlasting
Till my last heartbeat sounds?
Must these chase me fiercely like
A pack of ravaging hounds?
I need freedom! Give me freedom!
Freedom from these howling thoughts;
Free my veins, O! Free my arteries!
Clear these of those damning clots!
Let my mind not think of you,
Let my mind not pine,
Let my eyes not shed their tears,
Let my voice not whine.

Let my heart not wish to feel

Let my soul not crave

The presence of your form and figure

Even in my grave!

ALAS! THE ERROR

Thy sunshine shows me every morning

The path on which to tread,

Yet I know not why, I know not how

I always err instead.

I choose the way where others whisper:

"All your pleasure lies!"

To find at last, in search of pleasure,

I've lost my priceless ties:

My ties with You, my ties with peace,

Mt ties with the soul and mind,—

For I have, by the time I spent,

Left these all behind.

A frantic urge then impels me

To turn around and run

And reach the spot from where I had

Years ago begun.

By the time I reach the spot again,

I find the sun has set

Leaving me in the darkness where,

In sunshine, we had long back met.

ALL FOR ME

Serenity breeds when I have none

Either to love or hate

In solemn silence all alone

Without a foe or a mate.

In that world of silence is my peace

Where I'll be quarantined;

There I find my semblance, Lord,

Throughout my heart and mind.

Enter in my soul, O Lord,

With all that seem divine

And free me from this painful state

Of restlessness of mine!

Free me from my lusts and cravings

Latent in my poise;

In order that I reach Thy kingdom,

Give me a chance, Lord, give me a choice!

And void of all my human bondage,

A vacuum shall be made

To draw You in my soul where all

Human passions fade.

Here I stand, Lord, open-breasted

And all for You, I'll be;

And there You are Lord, open-armed,

All for me, yes, all for me!

THE AMALGAMATION

When my existence with all its glamours

Its success finds at last,

My present glories tend to merge

With the tears of my past.

Every action seeks its roots

In the failures of my life

And success traces its arduous paths

Of struggle, strain and strife.

And the soul seeks its fulfillment

Through future actions where

The past and present blend themselves

Virtually everywhere.

And in every action, I find, O lord,

Thy omnipotence is cast,

In the fantastic amalgamation

Of the present, future and the past.

AN INVITATION

Sensitive I am to every motion

That the earth generates

Through all its wonders which open wide

My thoughts' floodgates;

And ere I could realize the tumults raised

Through the sounds and lights and sights

Which sway the depths of my mind and soul

With a thousand and one delights,

I find my passions already moulded

More than I ever knew

As harbingers of peace and harmony

To love the world and You.

Come therefore and walk with me

Through the lights and shadows cast

By the foliage spread out all around,

And find your peace at last.

Come therefore and play with me

Through the woodlands and the glens;

Lie with me on the grass and greens

Where the woods are dark and dense.

Bathe with me in the waterfalls

And also under the sun

And see how all your charms will be

In divine magic, spun.

Come, dance with me and drink the nectar

Poured from the open skies,

For here lies all your peace and freedom

And here our pleasure lies.

AND I SHALL NOT RETURN!

This is when the phantom hours

Resurrect themselves into shapes

And brings to life the formless world

Through which my soul escapes

From the mortal world of shape and form

Into the mystic world unknown

And merges with the ancient genesis

Where the first of its seeds were sown.

And I am lifted like the clouds up there

In the endless span of skies

And trace my way through the Milky Way

Where all the wonder lies.

Let my condemned tears and laughter

Fade away through time,

For I have found my satisfaction

To make my soul sublime.

This is where my access means

Nourishing food for my entire soul

In a realm which lies far away

From the earthly chaos and rigmarole.

Let me leave in the earth's trash-trays

My consecrated urn,

For I have found my peace and content,

And I shall not return!

AND THE TWAIN SHALL MEET

In the chaos and unrest of this world

Somewhere the twain should meet

And the divine and the devil should

Unceasingly each other greet,

Where the devil shall be absorbed in

Whatever is divine

And the divine in its own wisdom,

Within the devil shine.

Let us meet then, Lord of Lords,—

Let me meet You there,

Where the worst of worst in my soul

Finds its thoroughfare.

Let me raise the worth of mine,

Let me purge and purify

Every nook and corned where

My soul shall sin and sigh.

And sin I must and sigh I must,

For I am a man indeed;

And merge I must and mesh I must

With Thy divinity's everlasting lead.

THE ANGEL'S TOUCH

Oh, this immense pleasure just to feel

And think of you in terms of what I gain

And what I lose in life, and being dissatisfied,

Turn to you and look back again.

This itself is an exercise which draws me near

The air I breathe, the water I drink and the gifts

Which you have given; and the tragedies and sorrows

With which my soul, itself in newer realm lifts.

And the oscillation in life throughout its course

Once towards what is good and then towards the bad,

Makes me understand and appreciate what I have

And differentiate it from what I had.

I have the sunshine, hills and oceans,

I have the entire earth for free,

I have my eyes, my ears and thoughts

To absorb all that I feel, hear and see.

Could I ever ask for more

Even when tragedy strikes,—

Could there be any difference drawn

Between my likes and dislikes?

For you have embalmed my sufferings

Which traveled from bad to worse,

By covering these with the layers of

The marvels of your universe.

THE ART OF LIVING

Would you ever call me Darling

Through the music of your lyre

And beckon me to step down at once

From the golden throne of my empire?

Would you ever find yourself

Happy in a state

Where you walk with me while I am

Bereft of my life's estate?

Would you hold my hands when I

Stand barefooted on the streets?

Would you come and kiss me when

I can hardly meet my needs?

Would you ever pull me down

From the achieved heights of fame

And make me face the painful world

Where poverty plays its game?

If you have never favoured me

With any one of these,

You have not made me learn

How to stand at ease;

Or how to understand what life

In rightful earnest means,

Through all its ups and downs

And all its diverse scenes.

Hence pull me down and make me walk

Through thorns and thickets where

Life should bleed in pains and tears

And be seasoned everywhere.

And accompany me, Darling,

And you will thereby find

That the reality of the entire world

Shall unwind.

THE ASPIRATION

Long ago I dreamt of wishes

In wings, like rainbows, clad,

Which remained ever unfulfilled

With nothing good to add.

Still I went on dreaming through

Days and nights and hours

Knowing well that all my dreams

Shall die like drooping flowers.

For me, however, my dreams were dreamt

For the sake of dreaming only,

And filling my soul with charming hopes

When I was feeling lonely.

And that is how I spent my life

For years together in the past

Never knowing what was there

Stored for me at last.

But I continued to dream all absurd dreams

Through quiet moments all alone,

While time flew through its usual course

With motions of its own.

A time had come when I had once

Myself and my fate condemned,

Till my ardent wishes to be paired with you

From my absurd dreams had stemmed.

And since then onwards, I had aspired

To have you as my lifelong mate

And cure the damage which I had suffered

Through the curses of my fate.

This was the sate of affairs when

Out of nowhere from the earth and skies,

You revealed yourself to embrace me

So lovingly before my living eyes.

My dreams are somewhat different now

With the touch of a legend or a lore,—

I dream of you in your earthly forms

And I aspire for a little more!

AT THE CROSSROADS

In the universe where Your greatness holds

Its awe-inspiring sway

And retains every form and matter

And guards them on the way,—

Draw me in and give me room—

A speck of space would do—

To mesh and mingle and to be

Unidentifiable through and through.

Draw me in and absorb me

In the colours of sunshine,

In the soft-lit hues of the moonlight and

In the universe's ending line.

Absorb me in the fathomless

Waters of the sea;

Absorb me in the grains of dust

And through eternity.

Crush my mind and body with

Time's endless span;

Stretch my soul and spirit from

The time when time began.

Spread my ego and my thoughts

Through every star which lights

The skies; and every sun

Which the entire space ignites.

Remove every cell of mine

And strew them all along

The massive expanse of Your art

Your rhythms, music and Your song.

Cast my feelings through every being

You've given life on earth;

Make me feel as if I am,

In Your magnitude, a worthy part.

And my realization shall be complete

Irrespective of whether I live or die,

When we shall have understood each other—

Just You and I!

You through Your greatness;

I through my humility,—

At the crossroads of mortality

And eternity!

THE BAPTISM

Everywhere when I search for life,

I stand face to face with death;

And everywhere when I search for death,

I confront life instead!

Life and death and death and life

Seem to merge in one,

Half of life is lost in death

And half of death, in life is won.

Marching in their own glories,

Both shall draw and wield

Their shining swords of ageless power,

And none shall ever yield.

As their game goes on through endless time,

Man pays scanty heed

To the inner urges of the soul

Pleading peace to take the lead.

Peace, ah, peace,—a mighty word

That's rarest of the rare,

Hardly found in the glossary

Where human actions dare

To invade the earth with lust and fire

And spoil the gifts of God

And smilingly opt for shedding blood

With the cudgel and the rod.

My vision's blurred and mission's marred

As I slowly travel through

History's tracks beneath my feet

Where I fail to find a clue

To enter the world where life and death

Shall glorify my basic human sense

And help me draw their graceful meaning

And baptize my existence.

BEYOND THE BORDERS

Clear and distinct through the air,

I heard you call my name;

I opened wide my drowsy eyes

To be involved in the game.

I called back, but then there was silence

And I felt drowsy all the same,

Just to be awakened and raise my ears

To the voice which again called my name.

In the moonlit shadows dancing here

With the trees and shrubs around,

The physique is not really clear

As much as is the sound.

It pierces through my heart and soul,

It churns my passions into lust;

It makes me forget who I am,

It levels my ego with the dust.

It burns my spirit with the love

Which no mortal ever felt before,

It lifts my fancies high and higher

Than heights where the eagles soar.

Unearthly, yet so sweet and charming

Is the voice which calls my name

And resounds through my soul and body

To light up my passion's warmth and flame.

How I wish to dress such voice

With human flesh and bones

To see for once, the woman who

Is the owner of such tones.

Perhaps a lovelorn hovering soul

In search of a mortal mate

Goes on calling, goes on calling,

To announce her abrupt fate—

A fate which might have led her to

Close her eyes forever, and

Forever crave some love and passion

Which she was never made to understand.

I give her therefore, every night

Audience of a lover while

I feel the pains which love may beget

Which took away her peace and smile.

The Birth of Poetry

When you had rejected love's advances

And dealt your cruel blow,

Poetry came to me and said:

'Darling, I have come to show

My inner beauty which you may

Feel and touch and taste

And embrace me in every form

So that none of us goes waste.'

Poetry then with all her charms

Bared herself and held

My arms with all her magic spell

While I withheld

My breath; and out of breathlessness,

As I stood in awe,

Was born

Love's everlasting law:

'Love begets pain

And that pain is sweet,

Matched for each other

On a rugged street.

And that is how

Love returns

As the cycle of pain

Full circle turns.'

And that is what

Poetry said,

While you left me alone

And I had bled.

And that is how

Poetry healed

All my wounds

Which now are sealed.

And that is where

Poetry brought

Peace and comfort

To a life distraught.

And that is why

Poetry must

Be your life's

Golden crust.

Let therefore your love's advances

Be rejected so that the pains

Could give birth to your poetries

From your ruins and remains.

THE BRIDGE OF SILENCE

Speak, but speak out softly though,

The songs your spirit sings

As Lady Silence lifts you gently

On her wide and soundless wings.

Feel how all your senses vibrate

With the thrusts which raise you higher

In the altitudes where peace alone

Is the only other flier.

Down below, if you cast a glance,

You'll shed your tears to see

War and hunger, discriminations,

Murder, hatred, poverty.

Shorn of all such selfish seekings

In the world which lies below,

You will cleanse your soul in earnest

In the heights of the Godly glow.

And as you travel high and higher,

There will be reasons enough to purify

Your soul and spirit through the links

Of silence, where all pleasures lie.

Anchored deep in the sea of silence,

Your soul shall find its golden hue,

Throbbing with a better life

And imbibed with a better you.

Enriched with all that are good and worthy,

As you will then descend

On the world of man where strife and conflicts

Never seem to end.

Gift us all your wealth and wisdom

Gathered while you strode

Along the bridge of silence to which the wretched

Never found the road.

<u>BRIDGING THE GAPS</u>

Now it is time that I must talk

With the words my poetries speak

And try to bridge the gap between

The genuine and the freak—

The gap between the wars and peace,

Truth and falsehood and

The gap between all human actions

Which I do and do not understand.

And my poetries speak to me in silence

Of life and death, of love and hatred, while

I try to bridge the gap therein

With my tragedy and my smile.

The entire world which stares at me

Is a story of fissures, gaps and rifts

Where I stand forlorn with my poetries

To stall and bridge the drifts.

And I talk with the words my poetries speak,

And I lift my passions from deep within

And inhale the strength to bridge the gaps

To find perfection in an imperfect scene.

And that's when all my inner senses

Rise together to raise

All that's lovely, pure and charming

In a toast to my poetries' praise.

And one by one, through the tracks of life,

As I cross the racing laps,

My thoughts are fine-tuned as I seek

To bridge the gaping gaps.

THE CALL

Just like this my days shall pass

And burn to cinders all

My expectations that someday I

Shall hear Your sonorous call:

The call of grandeur, the call of class,

The call from that wonderland

Where You and I shall someday meet

And each other understand.

The magic call which I am yet

To hear through my human ears;

The call for which our mankind waits

Since a hundred thousand years.

The call in pursuit of which all men

Worship You from birth

Since the genesis of civilization

Carved out on this earth.

But I have failed to hear Your calls

When thunderbolts have struck

The earth with all their awe and wonder;

And thus have missed the luck

To sense Your calls in thunderstorms

And sounds of hails and rains

Where mortal attachments disappear

And Your presence, Lord, remains.

Your voice beckons in thunder

And Your revelation finds forms

To be understood, seen and sensed by all

In rains, hails and thunderstorms.

And henceforth my days shall not pass

With expectations lost in doom,

For I'm now ready to hear Your call;

I am ready to see Your flower bloom.

<u>CATCH ME IF YOU CAN!</u>

My fascinations and fancies often find

Expressions which no man can share,

And that's the reason why I'm alone

In the realms where I fare.

My exultations through my onward journey

Are meant for me alone,

While my heartbeats send out rhythms of

Music which is my very own.

I bask in the sunshine of my life

After bathing in its ruins;

It loses nothing as it lost its all;

If it gains something, it wins.

The beads of thoughts which bind my mind

Are absurd, weird and strange,

Struggling for emancipation, yet

When unleashed, rush beyond their range.

My life has gamboled through the times

Garnished with its whims

While I have either cursed my partners

Or seemingly sung their hymns,

In course of which I have but only

Garlanded myself with bliss

And felt so peaceful all by myself

Without a caress or a kiss.

And these pour out my expressions

Which grace me all the while

And with my wisdom, stare and gaze

At the foolish world and smile,

As no one shall be ever able

To read and share my thoughts

And understand me in my entirety

By joining all the dots.

CHARMER! YOU HAVE CHARMED MY LIFE!

It's quite cold now after the rain is over

And there's a fragrance in the air,

Of moistened earth and the scent of flowers

While I am set to bare

My soul to give you access, Charmer,

And feel the magic which you hold

In your treasure-chest since ageless time

Where countless mysteries lie untold.

The burden of my work on earth

Is yet so incomplete,

And I have still to conquer miles

With tired, bleeding feet.

And in between I need break

To explore all the charms

Born and pulsating as of ever

In the magic of your arms.

And that is why these rainy nights

Send shivers through my spine

As I absorb the splendours of your passions

And make my Self divine.

Likewise, when the days are sun-filled

And the sky is bright and clear

Or when I travel through the hills and fields

And fill my heart with cheer,—

I explore your charms in awe again

And stop to take a break

And delve within me to taste the splendour

Just for splendour's sake.

Charmer! You have charmed my life

With all your magic treats;

Charm me likewise when I shall

End my earthly feats.

Charm me when I'll rise again

Beyond the Death-divine,

Just as you have charmed my life

And made it superfine.

CLUELESS

You have not yet answered where

My mystic provenance lies

Through grotesque grottoes of my life

In dire need of styptic dyes.

You have never granted me

The wisdom of the sage

To read Your mind and see in You

My very own image.

I have questions—a hundred thousand—

To which I've never found

A single answer from Your end

Or a single streak of sound.

The rainbow which I see here now

Reaching the horizon's end—

Are Your answers to be found

At the bottom of the bend?

Or do these answers lie amassed

In the thick black thunderclouds?

Or must these answers be sifted from

The gushing waters in the river mouths?

If I had but just a clue

To solve the crossword of my life

To find out what my end would be

And how I at all, did arrive—

I would have then seen in You,

My image, my very own,

And raised myself at par with You

To sit beside Your throne.

THE COLOUR CONNECTION

I wish to see you through these colours,

I wish to see you smile

Spread out all through nature's bounties

Gleefully all the while.

I wish to love you through these colours,

I wish to say : "I care";

I wish to make you feel my presence

Through colours everywhere.

Sorrow shall here find a place

To weep with sensuous joy

To cherish memories of those departed

Lest time should these destroy.

My system draws in all these colours

Through the scent I inhale here

And makes a coloured marvel of my soul,

This part of the year.

Let all these flowers blossom then

And colour all that's colour-shy

To make this world a better place

To live, love and Oh yes, to even die!

COLOURS—THE FINAL BLEND

If there were a hundred colours to my life,

I visualize them when I am alert

With eyes wide open, as I savour

The marvels of this earth:

Marvels concealed in black and white,

In yellow, red and green and blue

And marvels concealed in my joy and laughter

And in my sorrow, tragedy and my rue.

In all these colours I find a reason

To marvel at my happiness or my pains

As destiny tosses me on life's horseback

And once tightens, once loosens the horse's reins.

Every colour whether bright or dismal

Paints my life with misfortune or good luck

And swaying in between, I accept all

To find a place where a balance can be struck.

I remember now, when I was just a child,

How I marveled at the blocks of paints

Set within my painting box

Where a child's dreams descends;

And how I mixed the colours all together

To marvel at the common hue

And stared in awe at the final blend

Which was the resultant thus brought to view!

Years thereafter, now when I

Am a man with a seasoned mind

And the colours derived through my life

Are distinct and well-defined,

But need to be mixed and merged together

To find their balanced blend,—

I mix them all in God's empire

And find life's correct trend.

THE COMBINATION

In the obscure hinterland

Of every human art,

Your omnipotent sovereignty

Plays the leading part.

For every work I perform,

For every masterpiece,

You are the wizard, Lord,

Holding the supreme keys.

Even where I fail to see

Perfection in my work,

You Lord, tiptoe to ensure

That I fail to reach the mark.

You are the bizarre creator

Of the evil and the good

And the royal dictator

Of the 'should not' and the 'should'.

Punish not man for his earthly guilt

Nor reward his performance,

For man is but a puppet in Your hands

Shorn of all defence.

And You are the unique synthesis

Of all that's good and all that's odd—

The finest combination

Of the Monster and of God!

THE COMPLETE SEARCH

I need no money, but I need

Something precious to fall back on;

And throughout this wretched life of mine,

The search goes on and on.

I need no fame sure, but I need

A place to sleep and rest;

And throughout the moments of my life,

The search has failed its test.

I need no rankings, yet I need

To know the urges of my soul,

The search for which has never reached

Its long-desired goal.

I need no company, but still I need

Someone in my need,

The search for whom has proved abortive

And wrenched my heart to bleed.

I need no blessings, yet I do need

Peace in all its forms,

The search for which has lost its course

In life's thunderstorms.

I need no audience, yet I do need

To search for the owner of the voice,

But the search has failed and I have lost

My chances to rejoice.

I need no vision, yet I need to see

Your existence in all;

My search, alas, has yielded nothing

But a blind man's constant stall.

I need no nothing, yet I do need

Something I really know not what;

Something perhaps, which would prove to be

Of the slightest yet of the greatest worth.

None I need hence, save You alone,

To make me always smile

And my search is complete when You sprinkle

Your love for a little while.

THE CONFRONTATION

I want my life to flow like a river

And end up in the sea

And forget all the nuances of

'To be or not to be'.

I want my life to feel the touches

Of both sides of the banks

And hear the tunes of grief and joys

Spread through all the human ranks.

And as I travel through my course,

Let destiny rule my cause

And both in happiness and in tears,

Let me offer the same applause

To the Maker of my soul and body,

To the whims and logic of the Power

Which fills me both with hopes and despair

Through each oscillating living hour.

And as I flow on, let me absorb

All that's good and bad;

All that's lovely, all that's ugly,

All that's happy, all that's sad;

All that's pious, all that's evil,

All that's condemned, all that's blessed and

All that's sane and all that's insane

Created by Your glorious hand.

With all these enriched burdens, when

Life shall someday meet the sea—

Endless, vast and awe-inspiring

Beckoning me to eternity,—

I shall release all my burdens

And embrace the universe

Where all my sensual pains and pleasures

Shall disperse.

I shall stand then, face to face

With the graceful Ultimate

And reach the aspired final end

Of the age-long arduous wait.

My soul shall behold the birth of peace

Where life and death in lovelock lie

And kiss each other with maddening spree

Where one the other can't defy.

SIGHS

If you had feelings, you would have felt

My spirit's dents;

If you had eyes, you would have seen

My anxious trends.

If you had ears, you would have heard

My painful sound;

If you had legs, you would have been

Me-ward bound.

If you had arms, you would have come

To hold my arms indeed;

If you had charms, you would have lent

Your grace for a quiet meet.

If you had a heart, you would have kept

My image locked within;

If you had a mind, you would have framed

My shapes therein.

If you had desires, you would have known

Deprivation's writhing pains;

If you had affections, you would have shown

That it subsists and still remains.

And overall, if you were you,

You would not have changed

And everything would have been in order

And not thus disarranged.

THE CONSECRATION OF THE SOUL

Consecrated by your condemnation,

Undaunted I lie here on the road

Which leads to the portals of your Hell

Where I shall blissfully sing your ode.

Blissfully I shall dance with pride,

Peacefully I shall live

With a seasoned soul with which I can

My divine joys retrieve.

A soul which is made so sacred by

Your damning curses which

Refined all the soot and sins

And made my bearings rich,

Is a glorious gift with which I shall

Cleanse the Inferno of its ills

And absorb in my depths within,

All the toxic spills.

And thus my soul shall fill itself

With Hell's putrid waste

And be born again with flesh and blood—

Sinful, morbid and unchaste.

I shall again be condemned then,

In course of which again,

My soul shall find its consecration

Through your curses in disdain.

Thus again my soul shall rise—

Cursed but consecrated,

And in You, it shall find itself

Fully reinstated.

THE DANCING PARTNER

I can feel life dance in me

As much as I can feel death dance

To the weird and shocking tunes of God

Where destiny rules and rules out chance.

Foxtrot, tap or waltz or tango,—

With or without an aiding band,

Or any dance you may conjure

Where life's partnership with death must stand.

Life shall lifelong quietly wait

For death to come and pair

As a dancing partner, so that each

The other's perfection could share.

Life and Death must therefore hold

Each other in embrace

So much so that each shall find

Completion through the other's grace.

As this realization throbs in me,

I can hear Your distant call:

"I am Life, I am Death,

I am one in all."

And the voice vibrates in the air

And through the mountains and the seas;

And the flowers in my garden wither

And new flowers blossom in the breeze.

DEATH? REALLY?

Death does call us every hour

To remind us of life,

And makes its presence felt in silence

In existence's hive.

And as we mount the steps of years

And pass through seasoning time,

The thought of death does colour life

And makes it graceful and sublime.

If mourning can but grant us strength

When death dictates,

There should not be any reason why

We'll not surrender to our fates.

Let us view life just as life,

And view death just as death

And nurse the notion that our soul

Bridges both instead.

And the inquietude latent in us all,

With the genesis traced in fear

Of death, shall dissolve in ignominy

And forever disappear.

And life shall flow, as it always must,

Like a gushing river, where

Force is matched with strength and beauty

And injunctions thrown haywire.

And there lies all the charms of death

Which provides life's delight,

Just as darkness always lends

The charms concealed in light.

<u>DEDICATED THOUGHTS</u>

Just because I thought of you

When the weather had been fair,

That's why you have carried me

Through the days of my despair.

Nothing seems to me to have

Ever been impaired,

As I resurrect myself from the darkness

Where none had ever dared.

If fate had ever pulled me down

Through hours struck with gloom,

I knew, it was your modest calling

To endow me with the finest bloom.

Here and everywhere in life,

As I am hurled from time to time,

I find the chance to think of you

And make my entire life sublime.

And that is how I'll view my life

With unceasing sacrifice,

For there I feel your touch and passion,

And there your presence lies.

If this was not the way I shaped

My existence since my natal year,

I wouldn't have ever drawn you near

And you would not have been here.

To my satisfaction and that of yours,

What I only wish to leave behind,

Is a little speck in the wilderness

Of humanity, that I had been true and kind.

DELAY DEFEATS

The more I want my rest in life,

The more You burden me

With loads enough to bear in silence

Your decree.

While darkness covers me in sleep,

I seem to find the end

Of all the tumults of my life

As my dreams descend,

Only to be refreshed again

As I wake up 'neath the sun

And find the day that's born afresh

Filled with work and fun.

And there You push me hard to plunge

Myself in the sea

Of endless work with a tiresome burden

From where I may not flee.

Every day is filled up thus

With the joy of work ahead

With the postponed expectation that

Someday I'll find my rest instead.

But when the day should really come

To be called up on the stands

To receive the award of my rest, I may not

Have any time in my hands.

Let not the rest which I deserve

Flit like a spectre or a ghost;

Let it be given to me right now

When I need it most.

DESPERATE CRAVINGS

Am I blasphemed in my life?

Or condemned for being born?

Or ridiculed by destiny's lurking devils

As an object of their scorn?

Who shall ever understand

The soul's greatest needs?

Who shall ever question why

The heart incessantly bleeds?

Let me therefore on my own

Seek my own redress

And resurrect myself on my death

And enrich my life afresh.

As the designs of a natural order

On the Zastruga always change,

With steady motions, I shall also

Allow myself to arrange

My own celebrations to mould myself

With eternity's specious world

In the quintessence of God's empire

Where tragedies lie annulled.

In the limitless expanse of the galaxies,

Let me therefore stay afloat,

And let my soul in fusion lie

Wrecking confusion's crazy note.

THE DETACHMENT

Now it is time again

To come out of my I

And detached, stand here all alone

Beneath the lofty moonlit sky.

Here in silence, I'm awake

While the entire earth is lulled

To sleep in peace; while I find peace

In the cradle of the world.

And my love for all spreads far and farther

Along its lust-less journey through

The poor and hated, shunned, ill-fated,

Till I meet my aspired You.

Let my love for all then spread its wings

Throughout Your universe

And weave its network all along

Its journey across the stars.

And let my soul stand face to face

With the conscience of my I

And reject outright all my bondage

With passion's clinging tie.

DIFFERENT STROKES

The freshness which has crept in now

In the season's spring-borne air

Stirs my soul with rhythms which

Merge with my finest prayer.

I find now that the man in me

Shuns its evil and its sin

And celebrate the joys of life

With all my kith and kin.

How I wish to treat all seasons

As if all of them were springs,

And draw in me the entire mankind

With the goodness of all finer things.

Here along the sylvan marvels

Let me be an extrovert

And pour out all my sensuous urges

And feel their unique priceless worth.

Let me lend my throat and songs

With the songbird's merry notes;

Let me send my mind out there

Where the clouded cluster floats.

I'll send my saltant heart to you

To share my pulse and cheers

And purge out all you hates and evils

And help your soul to you interiors.

There you'll find a different world

Merged with the fervour of the spring

Where angels of a different order,

Of peace and harmony, sing.

<u>DISORDERS</u>

Engulfed in utter chaos—

You and I,

In or seats in the earth and the heaven,

With mocking confusions lie.

You with all Your splendours,

I with all my pains;

You with all your bounties,

I, where nothing remains.

You with all your marvels,

Blessed through man's prayer;

I with all my goodness

Cursed through every layer.

You with all Your crimes

Pardoned by man;

I with all my wrongdoings

Stand my trial for You to scan.

Unconscionables in Your kingdom,

Unconscionables in my earth;

Disorders in Your genesis,

Disorders since my birth.

DISSENTIENCE

As I trudge along the weary miles

Of life's crude and chaotic coast,

I miss Your kindly proximity

When I need You most.

And by the time my feet had bled

To drain the fluid in my veins,

And the pathways I have left behind

Are smeared with my bloodstains,

You arrive

In Your regent style,

And lend Your hand and offer me

Your graceful smile!

While irony strikes

And man ridicules

Your discrimination

And Your rules!

In Your massive Godhead,

Your omissions disappear

As mortals render prayers

With awe and fear.

In the context of this logic,

You are brute

As You veil Your shortcomings

While man plays his flute

Raising melodies in prayers

Through immemorial ages

Sanctifying in ignorance

Your multifarious images.

Should there be a meaning

In Your madness,

I'll find some happy hours

In my sadness!

THE ELIXIR OF LIFE

Open your heart to one and all

And the realization shall gain the ground

That right here in the world of man,

A paradise can be found.

What else can then be my solace,

What else can fetch my peace

Save the pleasures which I find lie hidden

While playing on the crease

Of the field of life; and open the game

With a giant shot

To reach out to and touch the heart

Of every human God.

It's pleasing always to find that when

I open my heart to all,

Happiness rushes in through my

Heart's open wall.

Let my heart be open then

As long as it should beat,

And capture all the happiness

And feel and taste the treat.

Let me touch your heart and soul,

Let me lift my wings

And fly to you to quietly hear

What your spirit sings.

There lies the magic of my being

And the elixir of my life,

From where I derive, through utter chaos,

My urges to survive.

THE EMERGENCE

At the peak of life where success has

Been tasted, touched and felt,

In Your warmth and grandeur, Lord of Lords,

My pride and vanities melt.

And the rays which glisten from Your form

Dispel all my doubts

To confirm that Your presence, Lord,

Surrounds my whereabouts.

Thus when You gently lead me Lord,

From darkness unto light,

My mortal frame then subtly trembles

In ecstatic delight.

Now that I have shattered all

My glamours at Your feet,

Let me hold Your hands my Lord,

And from this world retreat.

Let me find my I in You,

Let us together merge;

And from our amalgamation,

Let a better I emerge!

THE EVASIVE

My mind is tired and the drooping eyelids

Thirst for sleep and rest

But every moment I'm kept awake

By the urge to lead the quest

For all that's new and all that's game

To fascination's wonderland

Where I must unearth all scattered marvels

And feel and learn and understand.

Here then all the joys of knowledge

Feed my tired mind

And lift my soul to heights of glory

Leaving my sleep behind.

When must I then have my rest?

When must I then sleep?

When must I then find my ease

And quietly brood and weep

For that what I have not yet found

In spite of all my scans

Through the realms of the mortal world

Where human knowledge spans?

I know that I have not yet found

Something which I'm yet to find;

Something which I crave in earnest;

Something not yet well-defined!

THE EXISTENCE

As I feel I hear your footsteps sound,

My breast in ecstasy heaves;

But I rush out to my lawn to find

The rustle of the leaves.

I scent the fragrance in the breeze

And hope to find you in the bowers;

But in course of searching, I find the scent

Is spread from all my garden flowers.

I hear some whispers, and in my joy,

Frantically I run to meet

My aspired you; but find instead

Gusty winds and a dusty street.

I sense some touches on my arms

And feel as if you had kissed—

Yes, my arms are wet, but this is due

To the smear of the morning mist.

I hear a bell ring somewhere, oh!

Somewhere in my mind,

That I have seen you somewhere, oh!

In nature, well-defined!

THE REAL AND THE UNREAL

Life for me would have been

Much more congenial

If the unreal factors hade not vied

With those which are really real.

And perfection in work and art

Shall hardly ever reach its mark,

If the glory of the real and genuine

Is lost in the depths of the unreal dark.

I have found the real in nature,

I have found it in my songs;

And more than ever, I am convinced

That that is where my soul belongs.

That's the source from where my spirit

Draws its living urge

And my expressions with verve and colour

Beautifully emerge.

And since the time when you have stepped

On the threshold of my life

To glorify the inherent lying in me

Unexplored in life's honey-hive,—

Since then I have found in you

The living reality, merged and spun

With nature, beauty and my songs

All together bound in one.

For you are real with all your realities,

While I have draped you with

My imagination, expression and my heartache

Where the light of life is lit.

Even the real in nature and my songs

Would be rendered meaningless,

If I ever lose the real in you

At the cost of the unreal trash and mess.

And so does every living moment pass

With thoughts of you, which adhere

Inseparably to my work and art

And enhance them to a higher sphere.

And hardly a moment passes by

Without a thought which speaks

Of you and only you in me

Casting all their glorious streaks.

And the more I think of you in earnest

Garbed in nature and my songs,

Perfection in my work and art

Sounds its finest gongs.

And the more I dwell in you, O Lord,

My ecstasies rise in spate,

And the more it seems that I have sealed

Your reality with my fate!

THE FESTIVAL OF SILENCE

Dance, dance, dance away your life

And dance away your death as well,

For the Festival of Silence

Rings the beckoning bell.

The breeze whispers softly while

The sunshine spreads its layers

And the earth rejoices in Your glory

With silence in our prayers.

The trees blossom into songs of colours

With the silent change of seasons

In silent motions all throughout

For unseen unknown reasons.

Feel the silence in your soul

When you offer love and peace;

Feel how silence surrounds you

When all your longings cease.

Silence! Let silence engulf all of us;

Let silence bare our mind

And unmask all our superficials

And lead us to the perfect find.

Silence—the password just to find

A heaven on this earth

And the source of bliss in the life of all

To fetch its finest worth.

Rejoice! Rejoice in silence as long as you

Ride your life sky-high;

And rejoice in blissful silence when

You are just about to die.

And from life to death and in between,

Hold silence in your arms

And waltz or trot or tap or twist

Without the beats of sounding drums.

And the Festival of Silence shall then usher in

The sounds of peace

And all the melodies which you wished in life

Shall be audible with ease.

<u>THE FINAL BLOOM</u>

'Let my resurrection on my death

Be raised a spiritual body Lord'*

And all that I have missed in life,

Touch, in death, the sweetest chord.

For I have searched for Thee in vain,

Everywhere, O, everywhere,

But my sins have pushed me back again

To the venue of the starting square.

And that is why, Lord, in my sins,

I have craved and yearned for Thee

And awaited the amalgamation

Of the Divinity and me.

And just as the waves of the mighty sea

Secure and care for the coral reefs,

Every yearning in my soul

Eternal vigilance keeps;

And washes away the viscid sins

To reveal all that I

Had held for Thee in silent prayers

Till before I die.

And my liberty is given to demand of Thee

To lift me in Thy hold

And let me blossom in my death

A hundred thousand fold.

(* **I. Corinthians 15:14**)

FIRE AND THUNDERSTORM

If a fire had been lit in me

By the friction of my pains,

If a thunder had been raised in me

By the storms which thrash my brains,

Would I or would I not indeed

Have found my pleasures set

Like diamonds in a world of nothing

Where I am left to fret?

Or like jewels which find their pricking place

On the chest of a lovely bride

Who smiles at me to smile with her

Keeping all my pains aside?

But still now, as the years pass by,

The fire has not been lit,

Nor the thunder even raised in me

To lend me the power and the grit

To overcome the wanton despairs

Following my footsteps through

The cursed pathway of my life

Paved with ceaseless rue.

But the fire shall be lit someday

And the thunder shall be raised

Just before I'll leave the world

When my body shall be based

On the fire which shall burn below

With the thunderous rising smoke

Echoing all my sweetest yet my harshest words

Which my soul and spirit ever spoke.

THE FOUNTAINHEAD

The winds shall raise my failing spirit

And the rains shall clean the coat

Of depression which has sought to cover

My mind's normal note.

The sun shall help to burn my despair

And the sea shall help to cool

My disturbed tracks and trends of life

Which were there so long to rule.

The earth with all its majesty

Shall lend its graceful strength

To lift my dwindling confidence

And brighten my existence.

The endless heavens with their massive stretch

Shall beckon me to share

The divine charms which they have spread

Throughout the earthly air.

The mountains with their solid stand

Defying time's corrosive tracks

Have given me the strength of standing

All alone through my mortal tracts.

The thunderstorms with their force and fury

Shall blow to pieces my weakness from

Every corner of my mind

By raising an inner thunderstorm.

What more then I need to plead

Before the mortal world of man?

For mortality can never deliver

What immortality, by itself, can!

<u>FRANTIC PRAYERS</u>

Once again now, more than ever,

I need Your guiding lights

To steer my actions in fairness through

These paths of great divides—

These great divides of man and man,

These great divides of ego clashes,

These great divides of colour bars,

These great divides of ethnic trashes.

In the regions of these great divides,

Your powers never reach,

Where man creates his own misfortune

With impunity and breach,

While You, a silent onlooker,

Powerless and dull,

Help to cover mankind with

A graveyard's grotesque lull.

When shall You then intervene

With all Your massive strength

To decorate the world with love and passion

That You had really meant

To gift Your creation from the Chaos

When the birth of the Earth took place

While You shaped Your Adam and his Eve

To give us the human race?

All in vain, Lord! All in vain?

But 'Let there be light!' You said;

Well, did You not in reality, mean

An enlightened soul instead?

Where Lord, where Oh, is the enlightened soul

To whom we may turn in times as these?

To soothe our pains, to heal our sores

And to cure all evils as You would please?

<u>FRESCOES</u>

In an obscure corner of this world

I derive extra-ordinary pleasures

By drawing frescoes of life

On the surface still so wet

With ordinary tears

Of an ordinary man

Bearing the beatings of destiny

In an arena where I've been thrown

Powerless against an omnipotent adversary

—My fate—which jeers

At me as I take the punch and fall

Flat on the floor; and ere I could rise,

I take the punch again; and the game

Continues till I may not rise again

And I close my eyes in pain;

And there lies concealed the genesis

Of my sweetest songs which find shape

Through the lovely art I see in life

And I paint frescoes of poetries of life

With the ruins which remain.

And from the shattered ruins then rise

Temples of mercy and churches of love

And abodes of peace where pains melt away

In history; where happiness is the order

Derived from the dark

And the gloomy; and the morbid past

Thrusts itself into oblivion; and the present

Is filled with calmness and contentment

Immensely satisfying to the soul

Where You embark

And spill Your presence just to heal

The scars and wounds which left their marks

While fate had taken its arbitrary toll

Upon a victim in an unequal battle,

But finally lost—

For the vanquished had risen from the ruins

And gathered the strength through pains

And painted frescoes of life to derive

The power to ignore the befallen tragedies

At a priceless cost.

FROM DARKNESS UNTO LIGHT

Now again these lonely hours

Are burdens on my veins,

And the darkest darkness of the night,

My only friend remains.

Here no stranger ever shall

Pierce my soul with stings;

Here I see no evils mar

A hundred thousand things.

Here I muster all my courage

To open wide my eyes

And see through all the darkness where

Your graceful image lies.

And as the darkness enters and

Dissolves within my flesh,

The vacuum's filled by the lights of wisdom

To know my self afresh.

Here then as the king of darkness,

I'll rule with a monarch's stride

And blend with the darkness all around

And wear its sheen with pride.

For the darkest darkness is a mighty friend

Who shows me the way to light,

And from the lowest depths of ignorance,

Reaps knowledge and delight.

Out of darkness, I'll seek and find

The light to ignite

The cognizance latent in my soul,

In the silent darkness of this night.

THE GARLAND

I am here to live with lonely hours

And find my happiness there

And weave a garland with my thoughts

And lay it where you fare.

And if you happen to walk along

The path where the garland lies,

Lift it darling, and wear it gently,

For there you'll sense our lifelong ties.

And someday when I shall forever depart

After my destined days are done,

Think of me and pluck the thoughts

From the garland one by one.

Think of the time we spent together

In the rains and thunderstorms

And our explorations in excess

Of daring norms.

Let memories revive

In life-like style

Where you can feel

My love and smile.

Through the garland of my thoughts

My affections shall stay

For you when my image shall

Wither and fade away.

And I shall find peace

In the abode of the Gods,

If you wear the garland

And pluck the woven thoughts.

THE GIFTS OF A HOST

The loneliness which surrounds me everywhere

Showers me with endless pleasure—

Celestial and divine;

And has given me the strength and power

To feel, to touch and to quietly absorb

Your gentle breeze and bright sunshine,

Your rains, your storms and your snows,

Fields and mountains and your seas

And your magnitude spread far beyond

This world of man, in the stars and the skies

And the unknown chapters of the universe;

And thus bring us closer and create a bond

Between my soul and the unfathomable vastness

Of all that contain You;

And ushers forth a meaningful significance

Of life, of tolerance, of sufferings;

All ending in happiness and pleasure

Derived from the understanding of the immense;

Of love, of sympathy and of compassion

As harbingers of goodwill and fraternity

When these are needed most

In the revelation of a recreated destiny

And resurrection of a life worth living

Where the Devil had played a sincere host.

THE GLORIOUS DARK

In the dead of night, when the world's asleep,

My thoughts surround

The living moments which failed to find

The daytime's light and sound.

Here then in the darker hours,

I find the sunshine smile

And the sounds strike a sweeter note

In my tearful sad profile.

The solemn quietness of the night

Breaks the silence of my heart

When all my senses spring to life

And make me at once extrovert.

In the dreary nights or darker days

Which help me find my peace and rest,

Melancholy with all its divinity

Ushers in the very best.

In the darker stages of my life,

I must therefore seek,

The best of colours, the best of sounds,

In Your game of hide and seek.

THE GREAT CONSOLATION

In the quietness of this lonesome night,

Silent, dark and deep,

Just when I have time to sigh

And time to cry and weep—

For all the failures in my life

And efforts lost in vain;

For friend with whom I bonded myself

But never met again;

For those whom I had once, O Lord,

Embraced in my breast,

Who now in Your kingdom, have

Found their peace and blissful rest;

For all my lonely brooding hours

Shorn of a match or a mate;

For all the solitary mourning which

Mark my sordid fate.—

And just when I have wept enough

And all my tears are dry,

And just when I have no breath left

Even for a single sigh,—

And just then in my despondency

In the lucid quietness of this night,

Your Lordly image weaves its shape

In its vital lucent light.

THE HOMECOMING

As the distance shortens 'tween You and me

Along my destined road

Where, since half-a-hundred years and more,

I most painfully strode,

I wonder whether at the end

I'll find Your welcome nod

And see in You the shape and form

Of my ever-aspiring God.

My pace is faster now that I

Seek to reach the final lap

And leave behind my tears and laughter

As histories in the mortal map.

Long ago, more than half-a-hundred years,

My incarnation brought me here;

And now my work is almost finished

And home is joyfully near.

Homecoming is always a pleasure when

The reception is sweet;

And in that anxious anticipation,

We shall someday meet.

And in the halo of such solemn thoughts,

Let me recline

And celebrate Your glory

Till we inseparably combine.

THE HOPE IN DESPAIR

Why are all these strings of mine

Burdened with an unseen load?

Why no music springs to life

As I walk along the charted road?

What makes my soul feel encumbered

And my spirit numb and dry?

What makes my trudging feet so heavy?

What makes my senses cry?

What makes my breast heave painful sighs?

What makes my mind morose?

Why does this nausea sting me thus

And inject its fatal morbid dose?

This is not my wonderworld

Where my spirit earlier roamed,

This is not the Milky Way

Where my life with fullness foamed>

This is but the underworld—

Hades—the devil's dungeon where

The lost and outcast and the sinful and

The blasphemed and the condemned dare.

And this is where a ray of hope

Faintly lends its hue

That my doomsday may be glorified

By a rendezvous with You.

<u>INCOMPLETE?</u>

Have I seen the best of life

Or am I yet to see?

Have I been the best of me

Or am I yet to be?

Have I met the worst of life

Or am I yet to meet?

Have I greeted the world of yours

Or am I yet to greet?

Have I found the goal I seek

Or am I yet to find?

Have I bound my self with you

Or am I yet to bind?

Have I shorn my self of 'maya'

Or am I yet to shear?

Have I heard your distant voice

Or am I yet to hear?

Have I swept the path for you

Or am I yet to sweep?

Have I wept since long for you

Or am I yet to weep?

Have I known your world by now

Or am I yet to know?

How far in this scorching life

Am I yet to travel, yet to go?

IS THAT WHERE?

I strode alone with a heavy heart

And silence walked with me,

In the pitch-black darkness of the night

I could barely see

The contours made by living silence

As silence held my hands

And embraced me to fill with joy

My life's barren lands.

Never did I feel before

That silence tastes so sweet

At the juncture where my solitude

And peaceful silence meet.

Is that then the place where I

Have searched so long in stealth?

Is that where You reign, O Lord,

Unseen and to be felt?

Is that the sacred altar where

I can feel and understand,

All Your marvels, all Your wonders,

And hold and kiss Your hands?

THE IMPRESSION

When the unborn day is still a foetus

In the encaged womb of the night

Struggling to shape itself and wriggle out

From the darkness and the plight

Of imprisoned hours, I await

In eager anticipation of a glorious birth

Of a newborn day, of light and hopes,

Of expectations, joys and freedom on this earth.

Here at the junction of darkness and of light,

Where the shimmering colours of night and day

Churn themselves in elegant splendours

Till the darkness gives away

And the sky bares itself in gleeful welcome

While the first of the sunrays land

At the end of the stretched out horizon

Like living dreams, I stand.

For a moment I forget myself and my all

As if standing in a trance

And happen to see Your sudden shape

As if through a passing glance.

I'm flung back again on earthly thoughts

And the moment disappears

But leaves its impression on my soul

To stay on through the years.

IN QUEST OF PERFECTION

What ecstasy should cause to raise such tunes

Every night through these unearthly hours

In the invisible linings of my soul,

As I stand here awe-struck under Your powers.

What addiction should force me night after night

To forego my sleep and ask:

'Who are You and who am I

And what is our ordained task?

Where lies the genesis, where lies the end

Of all these manifestations which unfold here

Of the massive workload of Your motions

Touching the farthest of the far, nearest of the near?'

And while the darkness in its pristine glory

Embraces me and every cell of mine,

I feel, while gazing at Your starlit skies,

The quiet touch of all that are superbly divine.

And somewhere from this darkness all around,

Your luminous shape itself moulds,

And every night, in solemn silence,

The finest charm of life unfolds.

And every night, my spirit dances

To the tunes of the universe;

And till perfection is attained in flawless terms,

I shall rehearse!

I shall rehearse!

THE INTERACTION

Just as the cooling monsoon showers

Find reception in my heart,

The scorching heat of the burning sun

Likewise finds its worth

As I revel in the blazing sunrays

And burn my worst of sins

And cleanse the darkness concealed in

The history of my genes.

Thus then I can view the world

With refreshed sense and sight

And offer with profuse abundance

All that I have inside.

Once I feel the joys of burning

My evils in the sun,

The act becomes a divine craze

Filled with bliss and fun.

So easily I'm then drawn in You

And secured in a place

Where both of us can interact

Through hours, nights and days.

And that is only what I need

To live my life with a meaning and

Spend my moments where we can

Each other amply understand.

<u>I SHALL NOT BURN!</u>

I know for certain that You wish

To extract all my best;

That's why You have put me to

The strictest acid test.

And in course of proving all my worth

And enduring the worst of worsts,

I have lost my golden part of life,

I have forgotten all my earthly thirsts.

I have burnt my life to cinders and

I have poisoned all my hopes,

I have given up the will to climb the stairs

And I've sought the downward slopes.

Peace played truant with my soul

And my rest was lost in restlessness;

And struck with a mismatched existence,

My life spelt out its worthlessness.

In every sphere where I had wished

To keep my footing firm,

I found at last the existence

Of a deadly virus or a cancerous germ.

And all these just to prove my worth

And pass Your stringent test

Of dedicating my precious living moments

And be divinely ever blessed!

In this way I have lost my strength,

And seen my own downfall,

And sighed away my precious time

And burnt my life and all.

And when after all this seasoning,

I'll glorify myself and earn

My restful death on the flaming pyre,

I shall not burn;

I shall not burn!

IDLE HOURS

These hours help me most to draw
Your image in my mind
As all my thoughts with revived fervor
Through time's corridors wind
Down the lanes where we have left
Indelible memories of the facts
Of life; where the mind so often
Unknowingly with pleasures reacts.

These are times when similar feelings
Touch the spirit while
Longings coated with your visions
Find their true profile.

These are moments which neither melt
In oblivion's decaying depths
Nor ever lose their stronghold through
Life's footsteps.

These are waves which splash the mind
With incidents which touch and bear
A hundred thousand marks which colour
My life in every sphere.

These are waitings which are charming

Through every delayed hour

In the expectation of your presence

Like a sudden summer shower.

These are passings of my time

Through awards of the finest gifts,

Where my soul with all its affections,

Towards your winsome spirit, drifts.

<u>THE REACTION</u>

I have mixed my joys and sorrows

And churned them in my soul,

And spun them like a spinning top

And made them twist and roll

And spurned them out with violent spins

To abandon me forever

And leave me alone where neither may

Lift my passion's lever.

What I am and what I'm not

Shall govern my lifestyle;

Neither joy nor sorrow shall

Shear me of my smile.

What I have and what I haven't,

Shall no more set my worth;

My flesh and blood and bones shall only

Hail my presence on this earth.

And I shall be a perfect man,—

Perfect in the sense

That I shall exist, yet I shall

Never feel my existence.

<u>IN LOVE</u>

I have fallen in love with myself

Through my solitary existence,

Where I applaud myself on my own

And savour my own essence.

I am seeking sunshine in my life

To ward off all that's gloomy, dark and void

And the sunshine tastes so sweet and lovely

For I have so long, the dark enjoyed.

The dark with all its pristine wonders

Wove its magic spell

Round and round and all around

Raising ecstasy in each living cell.

And the darkness in my solitude

Or my solitude in the dark,

Lies amalgamated with each other

While all my senses soon embark

On the world of charming passions where

I find myself in love with myself through

The journey from darkness unto light

Which makes my life so meaningful and true.

I need then nothing more, nothing less

Than the bliss and peace I find

By tasting all the goodness of

The pleasures drawn in the troubled mind.

Myself I then wipe my tears,

Myself I then heal my scars,

Myself I then veil my tragedies

And lift all painful bars.

In my own glory, I see myself,

In my own halo, I shine,

Ah! I have fallen in love

With the loveliness of mine.

THE IMMORTALITY

I shall some day disappear

Into the elements which had once

Given me my shape and form

And life in abundance.

My breath shall prevail in the air,

My energy in the sun;

My movements, in the skies and clouds,

My vision, in the horizon.

My words shall echo in the songs

Which the birds shall merrily sing;

My existence shall find itself

Borne in everything.

In the earth's crust shall my flesh and bones

Find their immortal remains;

My poetries shall be raised to life

Through sunshine and the rains.

The waters of the ocean shall

Reflect my sorrows and my grief

With which I had been struck in life

And found but no relief.

My silence shall be portrayed in

The calm before thunderstorms;

In the sounds of bursting thunders shall

My wrath and anger find their forms.

My loneliness shall be figured in

The range of mountains standing high

And silent through the ages as

Witnesses to time which passes by.

My happiness shall be revealed through

The happiness of every man;

And my being shall always be a part

Derived from the ancient human clan.

And scattered throughout the period

From the beginning of human antiquity,

Interspersed amongst the elements of the universe,

I shall be! I shall be! I shall be!

<u>INDECISIVENESS</u>

Thoughts which rise like smoke from embers

Burn my spirit's sheen,

As I feel the difference 'tween what I am

And what I once had been.

Man is indeed born free, but then,

As soon as his innocence, wisdom gains,

He finds in shock and dismay that

He is bound in destined chains.

And the more I advance through the ages,

The more I find in awe and pain,

That the entire system of Your world

Is crooked and insane.

My soul is mismatched more than ever

In the reckless games of men

Played to win by fatal strikes

By the sword and not the pen.

The background of Your social order

Tracks me like a hound

And chases me to thrust me into

A fearful stretch of a worse foreground.

And the question is raised to seek an answer

From every smoking thought:

Should I remain as I am or change myself—

Should I or should I not?

THE INVISIBLE TIE

I've come here in the usual hours

And floated through the breeze

And searched for you in the skies and rains

And the foliage of the trees.

I stretched my eyesight far beyond

The horizon's visual bar,

Entreating the elements of the earth

To tell me where you are.

I strained my ears to find out if

Your voice would reach me here

To feel your semblance in your absence

As much as I could persevere.

Right and left I looked for you

With anxious searching eyes

As if your arrival should, through magic,

With my aspiration, synchronize.

And as I called through the caves and mountains,

My voice was returned to me

Echoing through the unknown barriers

Where you are supposed to be.

As dejection prospered through my nerves,

And my coffee became cold,

I raised my cup, and while my lips

Touched the cup, I lost my hold

And spilled the liquid all around,

Which made me forthwith realize

That your presence must have filled my mind

With your seeking unseen guise.

This is perhaps the place where we

Have tied an unseen knot

At a junction which is the meeting point

Of man and God.

IN ANTICIPATION

It is unusually calm and quiet tonight,

As if the Gods have gone to rest;

Not a whisper, not a sound,

Sends waves through nature's massive nest.

Is tis the harbinger of a thunderstorm

Brewing in the northern skies?

A storm so furious as would wash

Away all morbid sins and lies?

A storm so raging as would cleanse

Mankind of its evil notes

And gift us all Your blessings, Lord,

And act as poison's antidotes?

If that be so, then let it be;

Let this uncanny stillness gain

The monstrous strength of sound and motions

Till only truth and faith remain;

Till only all that's good in man

And all that's sweet and beautiful

Drape our souls with their artistry

And make our lives and spirits full.

In every sphere of existence,

Let us hail such thunderstorms

To cleanse our dirt-filled crust and see

Our inner self with its splendid forms.

IN DARKNESS AND IN LIGHT

In the dead of night when silence reigns,

Why do I hear your call,

O Friend in life, O Friend in death,

O Friend of one and all?

On waking up I find but only

Darkness by my side

With a thousand broodings breeding chaos

Across the ruptured mind inside.

I sit up as if hypnotized

Till my senses strike, and ask

Why am I spending sleepless hours

Over such a trivial task.

Trivial, is it? Or is it not,

To find out why you call,

O Friend in life, O Friend in death,

O Friend of one and all?

Exhaustion now gains me over

And I tend to fall asleep,

But then again I hear your call

From somewhere far and deep.

I rise again in awe and frenzy

With ecstasy in my soul

And wait with patience in the darkness

As the sleepless hours roll.

Till a streak of light and still more light

Spread their coloured wings

And brighten up the dark and dismal

Where the guardian angel sings.

And in the crimson rays of the rising sun,

Now again I hear your call,

O Friend in life, O Friend in death,

O Friend of one and all.

<u>INSPIRATIONS</u>

To me, every hour brings anew

Freshness of a divine order

To fill me up with grace and fullness

And enable me to cross the border

Of life's emptiness, where I alone

Stare at you and convert my dismal days

Into moments of happiness sent by you

Through the brightness of the morning rays.

And hence I wonder, how you have

Refilled my vacant hours

With the marvel of your natures bounties

Gifted through the sun and showers,

Which spell your existence in all

And cover me with a divine sheen

To feel through all my mortal joys

And tragedies that you have been

Present with your omnipresence

In your Godly style

And helped me earn in silent motions

A quiet, seasoned man's profile.

What with all my joys and sorrows,

What with all these worldly thoughts,

When I have felt you hues in me

And seen and felt your beauty spots?

I'LL BE WAITING

The sounds of raindrops here on earth

Softly seem to hum

The tunes of my anticipation

That you shall come.

And with every drop of rain, I shed

My own drop of tear,

For I hear your sounds but find in pains

That you are still not here.

But this is the finest gift with which

You have charmed my life—

To wait for you in anticipation

And charmingly to survive.

For throughout the hours of my life

I shall wait for you

And feel the marvels of my being

Everyday anew.

Till someday when my soul shall rise

Above this mortal being, when I

Shall embrace you with divine greetings

And bid this world goodbye.

THE IMMORTALITY OF THE MORTAL

Now that all my tears are dry,

The vapours rise

To reach the kingdom where you reign

In disguise.

Now more than ever I do find

The meaning of my tears

In the mortal world where I have lost

My precious yesteryears.

For time never held its breath

To stop and pause

To speak a kindly word or two

For my cause,—

Nor shall time

Ever halt

To appreciate

Or find a fault;

But shall always pass

And heed no call,

And within its massive fold,

Draw us all.

And someone or the other

Must always be

Left alone in darkness

To mourn and be.

And that is where

Immortality finds life,

Where mortality means

To weep and survive.

<u>I SERVE</u>

It's daybreak now, and four-thirty,

Just before the sun

Should rise with all its glory from

The eastern horizon.

And I have feelings which erupt

With the grandeur of the dawn,

For here my spirit unto You

Is ecstatically drawn.

For here my soul is one with You

Where the quivering lights do shine

All across the skies to cast

The spell that spells divine.

How I feel that all my senses

Should spread out like your lights

And engulf the expanse of Your earth

From the oceans' depths and mountains' heights.

How I feel that all my actions

Should spread out like the rays

Of the rising sun which just by rising

Shows us what it says.

Let my work be meant for all

And let my actions find

Their fulfillment by serving Your

Treasured humankind.

IN SEARCH OF AN ANSWER

If ever I am struck by God's

Irrevocable curse,

And lose forever this gifted art

Of painting life with my poetic verse,—

And if you find my heart and mind

Stand still and petrified,

Shorn of all their powers to

Create what I feel inside,—

And if my soul then fails to respond

To the marvels of the earth,

And shies away from classics or

Equally from pain or mirth,—

If the sun and rains and thunderstorms

Do not strike their notes

In the damaged chords of my existence

Failing to decipher the codes,—

If the man in me that makes an artist

Is damaged to the hilt,

And my features which had drawn you near,

Are covered by soot and silt,—

If the beast which is dormant now in me

Bares its monstrous teeth,

And drives away the man in me

And springs up on its feet,—

If ever in my life I lose

All these, then,—then will you

Be the same as you are now

And come to my rescue?

Or will you then in hate and disgust

Spurn my altered frame,

And discard me for living a life

Of ignominy and shame?

<u>THE JOURNEY</u>

In the desertland where life is setto sail

Through all that's parched and dry,

And waste its glamour through the routes

Where devastations lie,

I am destined to live and smile

And forget my ruptured past

And hold aloft with hope and pleasure

Expectation's mighty mast.

In me you shall then find your mate

To sail through the troubled seas

And overcome life's untamed waves

Which never seem to cease.

In me you shall then find your pains

Dissolved in those of mine;

In me shall all your tragedies

With those of mine combine.

Where God is heartless and fate's a demon,

I shall be your friend

And together we shall find a haven

At the rainbow's oft-sought end.

Together we shall cultivate

The best we have in store

And rear the strength of divine power

Lying latent in our core.

And with this we shall face and confront

The tragedies of life,

And with the bloodstream flowing in our veins,

We shall survive.

And late in life, when we shall look back

At the events and revise,

We'll find that the desert we have crossed by then,

Has turned into a paradise!

<u>KNOW THYSELF</u>

Now that I have pushed some liquid gold

Down my thirsty throat,

Confusions are given a go-by and

Logic stays afloat.

Here I discern the God in the Demon

And the Demon in the God;

Here I receive my holiest sins

With a smile and a welcome nod.

The image of my goodness here

Is unmasked when I find

Hypocrisy staring at my face

Like an uncontrollable Frankenstein;

As if this nectar wields a magic

And holds me hypnotized

To purge out all that's meaningless

From the world which man devised.

Every sip of this golden liquid

Drives sanity in my frame

And the gnosis of the true and false

Hastens all my shame.

The more I drink this toxic liquid,

The poison acts to clean

The silts of poison which have choked

My purely human sheen.

And then, and only then I stand

With powers of divine span

To blaspheme or glorify

My image as a man.

LEAD! KINDLY DARKNESS

As the twilight fades out and the day

Disappears in the endless expanse of the sky,

All that are charming in your darkness

Are drawn in through my inner eye.

Idling away my time for nothing

Amongst a thousand jobs to be done

Is a much too precious a pleasure which

Is sought for till it's won.

For wisdom gains its expanse while

Salvaging light from the ignoble dark,

And while repelling darkness from its hold,

Knowledge finds its enlightened mark.

This is where your nightlong darkness

Shall be my teacher and my guide

And enhance all my traits of wisdom

To seek out the colours of your light.

And when I shall have but fully inhaled

The pleasures of all that are dark and dainty

And amassed wisdom in my soul

With proper breeding and aplenty,

I shall let the darkness of the night

Disappear through the dawn in the morning light,

And invite the sunbeams which then shall seem

Twice as sparkling, twice as bright.

LET THERE BE LIGHT!

Just at daybreak when the world

Is half awake and yawns,

Just when the first of morning lights,

Shyly, coyly dawns,—

And just when the streaks of light thereafter

Dispel the darkness of the night

And ushers in the first of sunrays

To the entire world's delight,—

There you wait with arms outstretched

To greet me with your glows,

There you are Lord, there you stand,

There my motion flows.

Let my being thus flow and reach

Your beckoning outstretched arms

And seek from you the lights of life—

The best of gifts, the best of alms.

In this manner, dispel, Lord,

Dispel the darkness of my life,

Just as the daybreak clears the night

And makes the entire world survive.

LET'S SHARE

Once again my passions mix

With nature's inevitable trends

When the full moon rises in the East

And the sun in the West descends.

And here when the twilight makes the earth

Obscure like a forgotten dream,

My senses clamour for your presence

To share the passing gleam;

To share the pleasures of this moment,

To share the beauty of this sight,

To share with you, my fancies through

This crepuscular delight!

Yet all my wishes sigh in silence

And let this moment pass

And end their glamour in this night

Leaving just a touch of class—

A touch of class, a touch of magic,

A touch of a dreamland in my eye

Meant to be shared by us alone—

Just you and I!

<u>LIBERTIES</u>

There's no harm in wishing to reach
Dizzy heights,
There's no harm in wishing to win
All your fights.
There's no harm in wishing to soar
High up in the skies,
There's no harm in wishing to find
Where the treasure lies.
There's no harm in wishing to work
Just for the sake of work,
There's no harm in wishing to run
Where others walk.
There's no harm in wishing to be
The very best—
Your ardent wishes and not the result,
Is the test.

LIFE, DEATH AND MAN

Where Death bares its monstrous fangs

Like a Hydra-headed brute,

Life sits happily in the land of hopes

And plays its melodious flute.

While every footstep advanced by

Death is charged with fear,

Life's rhythms pulsate merrily

In every conceived sphere.

And as Death beckons both life and the lifeless

To rot and decay through their fates,

Life, through its joyful passing moments

Delivers and unceasingly creates.

When Death emerges like a sniper

From its hideouts here and there,

Life shoots out with all its valour

Like a saviour everywhere.

Death is not a mystery though,

For its motionless and cold,

While Life is strange with gifted magic

With an ever-changing mould.

Death rides on Life's horseback

And whips it to tune,

While Life absorbs it as a seasoned sport

And renders itself immune.

And the world watches the crazy game

Unable to solve the ageless riddle

Why man should be flanked by Life and Death

And remain swaying in the middle.

LIFT ME

Lift my soul yet high and higher

To reach that coveted height

From where my conscience shall be able

To sift what's wrong or right.

Lift my thoughts to reach the realm

Where knowledge lights the light

Of strength and courage and of freedom

And to view my dark inside.

Lift my actions to reach the stage

Where I can nobly understand

Whether ego rides on life's horseback

Or tears are wanting in my ruling hand.

Lift my yearnings under the sun

On the altar of sacrifice,

To weep, to feel and cry for others,

And for the world, to wet my eyes.

Lift my senses high above

To reach that refined ground

Where all my drives in life and always

Should never run aground.

Lift me in your kingdom then,

When I have all throughout

Lifted myself in mind and spirit

And shed my selfish clout.

THE LONGING

Time has passed by, but still I have

Not yet found the time

To sing Your hymns and think of You

And make my life sublime.

And this is how my time shall pass

Every day and night

With the repentance that I have failed

To feel You by my side.

And this is how my work has been

Acting as my foe,

Stealing all my time from me

Up above and down below.

In work I have but charmed myself,

With excellence so well-defined;

But in course of working, I have left

All Your thoughts behind.

If working is a craze with me,

If its *yoga* is an art,—

Can it ever compensate

The longing of the heart?

LOVE'S LABOUR

When I wait for you through lonely hours,
My time does not seem to pass—
But stalls in wonder just to ask:
"For whom is your patience put to task?"
—"The touch", I answer, "the touch of class!"

When I pine for you in expectation
That sooner or later you shall come—
The silence emits a whispering sound
Asking: "For whom you look around?"
—"The feel", I answer, "the feel of calm!"

When I whine for you with loss of patience
And deprive myself of my ease—
The air around me voices queries:
"What's the reason which yourself wearies?"
"The wait", I answer, "the wait for peace!"

When I feel so restless all throughout
And struggle like a singled dove—
Do I hear from you afar:
"For you my arms are kept ajar,
I'm coming soon for the kiss of love!"

MAGIC IN MOTION

The sun is yet to rise and redden

The earth with all its lustrous might,

And I wait here with my anxious moments

To absorb the colours of its light.

The sounds of life have sprung to action

And the world is set in a welcome mood

Waiting with its throbbing beats

To greet your advent on its route.

Now again the colours splash

All along the horizon

As the veil of darkness is lifted and

Evil and ignorance are on the run.

And then with all its grace and glory,

Floats in space the rising sun,

And the finest magic of the heavens

Is on the world of mortals, spun.

Away! Away with all that are dark and evil!

To hell with ignominy, bondage and

Let us welcome knowledge, fraternity

And peace and welfare on our land.

THE MAGIC OF THE ARTS

An art in every golden sunray—

An art in the falling flakes of snow—

An art in nature's exhibitions—

An art in the master-craftsman's show

Holds me in rapt attention as I visit

The endless gallery spread out through

The massive expanse called universe

Where I've been called for an interview.

I've not been questioned to test my wisdom

Nor do I feel at ease

And I simply stare at all your marvels

Magnificently crafted such as these.

In silence and with stopping heartbeats

I see the snowcapped mountain ranges

And I thrill myself through the mix of colours

Varying as each season changes.

I see the timeless flow of rivers

And the unceasing matchless waterfalls;

I hear the sounds of crashing waves

And the gathering thunder's roaring calls;

And there again I find your arts

In perfect order crafted,

And every time-set worldly motions

In flawless wordings drafted.

And as I pass through the endless gallery

Of your arts and crafts, I tend to become tense,

And ere I am aware what's really wrong,

I seem to forget my existence.

And that's the moment when I hear

A distant voice—a question—at the interview,

Asking me in simple language:

"Tell us who are you?"

My throat is choked then and wisdom blocked

With confusions with which I never can

Answer, as I merge myself by then with you

And forget my identity as a living man!

THE MANIFESTATIONS

Like the stars which stud the entire sky,

Like the graceful beams of the full-grown moon

Which softly colour-wash the space

Where whitish flakes of clouds are strewn;

Like the gusts of breeze which pass by me

Invisible to my eyes,

Like the sky-kissed margin of the oceans

Where endless water lies;

Like the sunrays pouring down on earth

To make it sparkling bright,

Like the monsoon showers streaming down

Much to man's delight;

Like the greatness of all honoured souls

Touching the life we lead;

Like a good work done should influence others

And make way for a better breed;

Like a kindly word when softly spoken

Should break the stiffened mind;

Like the powers of the mind and soul

Should thrust all weakness far behind;

Like the finest art in every field

Is a source of pleasure for us all;

Like the dancer's moves, the singer's voice,

Or even the songbird's rhythmic call.

Just as all these on their own

Have cast their magic spells on me;

Just as I have sensed my pleasures

Through nature's artistry,—

Spread out through every cell of mine,

Is Your essence,

With its glorious manifestations

Throughout my existence.

THE MASTER'S TOUCH

The Master's touch with which You have

Added endless strength

To all my cells to ensure that

My endurance is lent

To work for You, is a classic gift

Which ensures that I raise

My performance to newer heights

While exhausting myself through my living days.

What magic, I know not, has been deftly

In Your art concealed

To revive all my strength and fervour

Should weakness cross the field.

The Master's touch—the touch of class—

Which guards this short lifeline

Makes this life worth living and

Equates it with the superfine.

Here then faced with all my burdens,

Tears and hurdles, all,—

I find my strength and confidence

Whenever I have to stall.

And within me, Your existence

Then finds a seat

And makes our nexus

Meaningfully complete.

THE MATCHING DIFFERENCE

In the intricacies of the network which

Life and death adorn,

Throughout the days and throughout the nights

Knowingly or unknowingly, I am drawn.

And the motion never stops at all

As I am hurled from end to end

With confusions galore where logic hardly

Ever cares to match or blend.

All my senses are kept alert

As I wend my way through unknown heights

Just to crash down far below

Where eternity is veiled and the earthly resides.

In the galaxies of ageless space

I search for answers but in vain,

To satisfy man's timeless query

To solve that endless mystic chain

Where two worlds of a vastly different order

Tend to amalgamate

And from opposite poles with mismatched forms

Create an apposite human state.

THE MEANINGFUL

When I try to gauge the worth and meaning

Of my being and existence,

On the touchstone made of beauty which

The earth her marvel lends,

The conscious feeling of that joy

To live in fullness this passing life,

Through every heartbeat in my chest

Is slowly brought alive.

And with the pain behind of having lost

Through the chronicles of time,

The sweeter part of my ageing life

Which could have turned sublime,

The marks on the touchstone of all that are

Good and beautiful,

Make the painful part of life indeed

Much more meaningful.

THE MESSAGE SHALL NOT DIE

Let me inhale in peace and freedom

The sweetness of your air,

Unobstructed, uninfluenced and in fullness

Throughout and everywhere.

Why then should this breathlessness

Suffocate my throat

And hold back the forward motions of

My life's sailing boat?

Should I have to stall myself

In the middle of the sea

Where there's nothing in the rear or front

Which my widened eyes could see,—

Give me strength and time, O Lord,

T o at least proclaim and crown

Your age-old attempt to ensure peace,

Ere my sailing boat should drown.

And the next soul who shall come a-sailing

And reach the spot where my boat had drowned,

Shall hear my proclamation clear and loud

Through the ocean's wind-raised sound;

And shall find the clue and sail along

Asking the world for peace

Till he should also find his end

Somewhere in the seas.

And the message shall be relayed over

Through and through,

And shall be kept alive to aid the heavens

By all of us and You.

<u>**THE MOMENT**</u>

If this is the song which I should sing

As the last of all my songs,

Just before I say adieu

To reach the kingdom where the soul belongs;

If this be the poem which I should write

As the last of all my joys,

Just before I leave this world

With God's envoys;

If this is the day which I should see

As the last of all my days,

Just before I close my eyes

With the twilight's fading rays;

If this is the breath which I should draw

As the last of all my breaths,

Just before I join the mortal band

Of so many other deaths;

If this is the art which I should raise

As the last of all my arts,

Just before the fatal hour

When life departs;

If this is the word which I should speak

Ass the last of all my words,

Just before my lips are stilled

As silence surrounds my vocal chords;

If this is the hour which I should spend

As the last of all my hours,

Just before my destined time

My existence devours;

If this is the thought which I should think

As the last of all my thoughts,

Just before my senses are

Sealed with blurs and blots;—

For a moment, let me be

A part of You,

And understand myself

All over anew.

<u>**THE MOTION**</u>

I seek my freedom from the pains

Which love has ushered in;

And my solace from Your holy image

Carved out from my greatest sin.

I seek my light from the darkness where

You have let me fall;

I seek my motion from the point

Where You have made me stall.

I seek my peace where warring thoughts

Pervade all my mind;

I seek to advance just where You

Pull me from behind.

I seek to rhyme my songs just where

Discords ruin my life;

I seek to find Your glory where

It's toughest to survive.

The sweet melodies of Your love

Become sweeter every day

With their untouched, unseen, unheard forms

Where distance lends its ray.

THE MUCH AWAITED

Where the mind is tired and droops like eyelids

On heavy, drowsy eyes;

Where nothing remains to be wished for further

In any shape or size;

When life has found its strength exhausted

Through vain attempts to match

Your tunes with those of mine in life

In the relentless matchless match;

Where the eyes have spotted the destined island

Of life's expansive sea;

When failing senses heave a sigh

That rest should nearby be;

Where the lust to fight is lost in fatigue,

Frustration and hopelessness;

Where strength fades out and the spirit seeks

Freedom from all storm and stress;

Where the turbulent waves of the mighty sea

End up crashing on the beach—

You stand there Lord, where I need rest,

Within my soft and easy reach.

You stand there with all Your halo

And all Your welcome and

Beckon me to sleep forever

In the much awaited land!

THE MUTINY

These bleeding wounds shall never heal

Nor shall they ever let me die,

But shall go on bleeding ever always

And all my hopes belie:

My hopes for finding a friend in you;

My hopes for a concerned mate;

My hopes for a world of peace and sojourn

Where painful thoughts abate.

The pageant here I see on earth

Crashes like a house of cards,

Where melancholy with all its glamours

The finest tunes imparts,

And makes me sway and dance with tears

Like a 'Nataraj' unbound,

Ecstatic in rage and pain

With every sight and sound.

No more I feel now that I am a man

Born to serve his God—

But a ruler of the universe

Swaying the ruling rod.

No more shall my hands now be

Folded with my prayers;

And love shall no more rush to seek

Its quiet and dainty shares.

For now in awe and wonder, really,

Your eyes shall have a feast

Of a sight of a weird combination

Of a man and a God and a beast.

THE OBLITERATION

Mystery shrouds the life of man

More than it shrouds his death,

For fate plays with the life of man

While in death it stops instead.

With every passing living moment

The fatal cradle rocks

And tosses man into uncertainties

Of pleasures or of painful shocks.

And the cognizance of the queer and curious

And the bizarre and the weird

Makes an uncanny history of the mystery

Which mankind always feared—

The fear of death, the fear of evils,

The fear of losing youth and wealth,

The fear of colour, caste and creed

And the fear of loss of fame and health.

These mysteries surface only while

The living hours pass

To end forever when man dies

And regains the thoughts of class—

The thought that he had made his life

A mystery with these useless thoughts

Till death came and obliterated

All his blackened spots.

OH, THE PAINS!

Fancies of a Master Tailor

Cutting me to size,

Season all my senses through

The streams from my tear-filled eyes.

My tears are precious for they are

Burdened with the pains

Which paint my life with diverse colours

And brighten what remains.

They light up all my darkened hours

As I pass through rough terrains,

And extract the finest from my sorrows

Where the Godly entertains.

Nothing, nothing, nothing ever

Shall fetch a better prize

Than the urge to see through tragic moments

And find Your peaceful paradise.

Thus Your image shall be drawn

In the restless soul in me

And amalgamate my entire life

With Your lasting divinity.

I'll take the beatings till awesome death

Shall lift my soul and rise,

While the Master Tailor's final cut

Shall shape me to my perfect size.

<u>OMISSIONS</u>

Lost in the world of imaginations

Where countless wonder-flakes

Float in the shape of aimless thoughts

While the weary conscience aches,

I seek the pleasures of my life

In the sunrays, rains and breeze

As I roam here without an aim or cause

To retrieve pleasures such as these.

I wander in these woodlands where

Nature has its store,

And as I draw my pleasures in,

My conscience pricks me more.

For I have inhaled the joys of life

Through all my surroundings

Oblivious of caring for

So many little things.

Little things like pressing you

Warmly in my arms,

Or kissing you with love and passion

While holding both your palms.

<u>ON THE CANVAS</u>

I must seek a better world

Where my feelings shall fructify,

And draw the rainbow of my life

On the canvas of my sigh;—

A better world where I can flourish

With the pulse-beats of my wants

Which set to motion my mortal senses

In the bizarre cosmic dance;—

A better world where I can master

My grief, my joys and all my emotions,

And spread my soul a million-fold

Through the mountains, earth and oceans;—

A better world where I can retrieve

The colours which I have lost

And paint my disheveled existence—

But, oh! At what an absurd cost!

A better world where I can confront

The Devil and the God alike

With the seasoned marvel of my sorrows

Which always seem to strike;—

And thus I shall be content with

The colours I shall choose,

As drop by drop, the flowing blood

From all my veins shall ooze,

Till a time shall come when age and years

Shall burden my flesh and bones

And my wrinkled hands shall find it tiring

To depict and paint life's fading tones—

And a day shall come when I shall be

Petrified and dry,

And draw my final portrait on

The canvas of my sigh!

And just when I shall proceed to

Unveil the portrait, Lord,—

I know, I know, I know for certain,

You shall descend and applaud!

<u>ONLY IF I COULD!</u>

O Fashion-designer of the universe,

O Style-maker to life,

Reveal unto me the art of creation

And the use of your chisel and your knife!

Ah, then, but do you really need

To use your tools as such?

Or just without these, like a wizard,

You simply need to touch

The life around with just your fingers

To raise the masterpieces

Of art and designs with their magnificence

Stamped on all your wonderpieces!

Designer now and designer always—

What incredible colour and crazy forms

Adorn both the living and the lifeless

Till time rusts all and age deforms.

Teach me for once your wizardry

So that I may be able to touch in turn

The living and the lifeless both,

To see beauty in all things I touch, return.

Let my pleasure of creating designs

Overflow in spate,

O Style-maker to life, O Fashion-designer,

Teach me to create!

Teach me to create magnificence,

Teach me to create all that's beautiful,

So that I may savour in ecstasy

The creation of the wonderful.

Ah! With the touch of a finger if I could

Beautify the world with peace,

That would have been my artistry

In the creation of a wonderpiece!

<u>OUR UNION—
IN QUEST OF A MEANING</u>

I have basked my soul through years

In the warmth of that of yours

And stationed myself where my mind

Restless thoughts abjures.

I have soaked my heart with pleasure

And filled its chambers with

Affections which you have kindly lent

Through my life's hectic length and width.

I have tuned my songs of life

Matching the tunes you play;

I have nurtured my living cells

In your array.

I have inhaled with my breath,

The fragrance which you spread

And injected into my corpuscles

The genesis which you have bred.

I have let my staunchest ego

Melt within your spacious halls

Where my 'I' disappears like a drop of water

In the gushing waterfalls.

This is where I am stranded though,

With my pleasures, bounties and my strength,

And left to ponder all alone,

What, to me, my life has meant!

THE PASSAGE TO OBSCURITY

Someday I must pack my passions,

Longings, belongings, all;

And spill them in the flowing Ganges

When I hear his welcome call.

The call which rouses man's latent beauty—

Much more glamorous, much more splendid than

The finest creations of the finest senses

Embedded in the heart of man.

Quietly I shall disappear

In the silence of the woods

And retire in the haven which

The mortal world eludes.

And ere you could ever understand

Or diagnose my disease,

I shall pass into oblivion

And my breathing life shall cease.

All my feelings which I had lent

And emotions held for you,

Shall be left behind by the soaring soul

To be treasured here in lieu

Of my presence shaped in flesh and blood;

Yet time shall never stare or stand,

But push me soon into mystic pathways

Of history's obscure land.

Nothing shall remind you then

That somewhere in between

The universe's cryptic birth and end,

We had met and I had been.

THE PATH TO DIVINITY

I must exhaust all my passions

With the fullest human urge

To draw in me the pleasures of

The feelings where my lusts emerge.

I shall fill the void in me

With vibrant rhythms of all that are

Superb, sensuous, classic and

Much above the normal par.

I shall dance to the ravishing tunes

Raised in the playground of the Gods;

I shall throw my arms around

All forms of beauty which life allots.

Myself I shall unmask truly

In every human form

And exert all my strength and power

Like a furious thunderstorm.

Like Ophion and the Northern Breeze,

I shall mate, but with dreams,

And there shall be the birth of Chaos

Raging on the seems.

And when I shall have fully attained

My satiety to my fill,

I shall part with all that's earthly

And retire from the drill.

And then I shall but seek my entry

Into a quiet corner of my own

Where I shall merge my Self with You

In a peaceful haven all alone.

And after I have had the taste

Of the finest feelings of my mortal best,

I shall shun these as stale and morbid

And turn to divinity for peace and rest.

THE PERFECTION OF LONELINESS

Many a time in cherished silence

I have wandered all alone

And searched for the meaning of life

Concealed in all I touch, feel and see

Through my happiness and sorrow,

My rise and fall and undulations

Of fate. Yet I merely found the whispers

Of the breeze simply enchanting me,

And the sunrays pouring powdered gold

In abundance on all; and graceful clouds

Floating across the vastness of the skies

Shaping themselves into dreams of fantasy;

And I realized that loneliness holds colours

To paint melancholy with the joys of life,

And render meanings, sweet and plentiful,

To chaos and discords within me.

These are times when the softest touches

Of the elements tend to raise and nurse

The greatest emotions, like a mother's hands

Nursing a new-born infant at its birth;

Like a caressing hand of a passionate lover

And the touch of the lips all over;

And here my loneliness derives perfection

Through its togetherness with the sky, the oceans and the earth.

<u>THE PLEASURE</u>

I like it this way, all to myself,

Lost in a world of my own

Far beyond my mortal peripheries

Within which my passions groan.

I crave for freedom, rave for liberties

And save for traveling through

All that's wondrous, all that's sublime,

All that contains You.

Once to myself, I'm content

With the simplest of my thoughts

To find my escape-route from plenty

Where life in luxury rots.

Here I am then all alone

With all my happiness drawn

Into the nucleus of my soul and spirit

Through my prayers in the dawn.

Here I find my loneliness

Filled with precious gifts

As life through the waves of passing time

Unto Your supreme Godhead drifts.

What more could I aspire then,

What more could I really wish,

Where my detachments in my loneliness,

My mortal longings extinguish?

THE POETIC BALANCE

Time it is now to seek my solace

In the poetries which have raised

My soul from the dryness of a barren life

Where fate had only phased

Devastation in its classic style

Where I must stand in awe

And absorb all the tragedies

And appropriate them to my human flaw.

For I am made of life and blood

To withstand mortal shocks

And take the whippings of my fate

And cross all stumbling blocks.

Once fortune smiled at me indeed

And made me rise and shine

But it brought along and gifted me

Misfortune as my Valentine.

And with misfortune I had danced away

My time through the Aegean Seas

Till the time was over, when I found

That she shall never cease,

But shall hold me till the day I die

For her unlawful gains

Where from the gutters of my misfortune,

Her fortune remains.

And that is where my poetries have

Played their kindly role,

To strike a balance in my life

Between the devil and my soul.

<u>PRAYERS</u>

Belief is merely a consolation

And nothing, nothing more;

Or is it linked with something unknown,

If not really so?

Why the should You not descend

On the wings of staunch belief,

And give me the much sought peace and calm

And the much aspired quiet relief?

Why then should you stud my fate

With obstacles which hold

My life to ransom; and then claim

A price that's more than its worth in gold?

I never perceived who was at all,

Or could be my Lord and Master;

But I know indeed in rightful earnest

That my fate is spelt "disaster".

I pray for You, I pray for me,

I pray for all and everyone,

But my beliefs matter little, really,

An unhesitatingly the world goes on.

And so on shall it go for ages

As time shall rush to reach

The uncharted future which has in store

A gift for all and each.

The gift—an answer to all doubts and queries

Within a compass, short and brief,—

How a balance can be struck between

Facts of life and mere belief!

THE PREROGATIVE

Once in a lifetime I must have

Your blessings showered on me

And demand as of my right and title

The happiness of being hassle-free.

Must You not then hear my voice,

Must You not then bless?

Must You not then lift me up

From this ugly chaotic mess?

Have I ever lost my faith,

Or if lost, thence regained,

And failed to praise Your omnipotence

Or have I ever feigned?

If these be not, then why must You

Wryly smile and wait

Till I reach my doomsday gifted with

A smouldered, burnt-out fate?

I must therefore wrench Your writ

To oust all odds and sighs

And make me heave my breath of peace

And win my coveted prize!

Thus win I must and surpass all

To reach and hold the ace

Where You shall with Your pride and luster

Lend Your Lordly grace!

THE PRIDE OF PAINS

The crown is precious which holds the head

High with success and with gains

Yet still more precious is the crown

Which weighs its worth with glorious pains:

Pains of failure, pains of despair,

Pains of raw distress,

Pains of a life which failed to blossom

In utter hopelessness.

And these are pains and agonies which

Suffer in silence while

In contrast elsewhere success roams

With a happy, content smile.

Happiness is not a burden but

Pain is a burden true,

With which you have to trudge along

Silently all through,

With words unspoken, songs unsung,

Tears unwiped and cries unheard,

As you mount the uphill path of life

To face the worst absurd.

And at the end of the journey when you are

Wrecked and shattered, Oh!

The joy of reaching the aspired rest

In the welcome divine glow!

Can gains and content ever fill

The desire latent in the soul

To search and find our aspired peace

Through the bleeding journey to the goal?

THE PRIZEWORTHY

Nothing has ever been in order

With me.

Nothing is in order and nothing

Shall ever be.

All expectations of success

Have run aground;

And that state of perfection

Shall never be found.

I've made a nuisance

Of my life

Where mess and disorders

Triumphantly survive.

My past was filled with chaos;

But even my past

Stares at my present

With eyes aghast.

This must be how

You cut me to size

To make me worthy

Of receiving the prize

Which I shall have won

When I shall depart

With nothing but the purest—

The truth that Thou art!

The truth that Your presence

Pervaded my all

Through chaos and disorders,

Through rise and fall.

THE PROMISCUITY

A blast of wind which brushed my face

With the smell of moistened soil,

Just now as the showers dropped

At the close of the day's turmoil,—

Speaks volumes stored in the archives of

The history meant for you and me

Which cruise through time and spread themselves

In the span of eternity.

Likewise shall the rays of the sun

Raise melodies all through time;

Likewise shall the thunders ring

Your bells through every clime.

Likewise shall the life on earth

Spray colours in the carnival

Of my life and being, and thus ensure

Your magic in my survival.

And my life shall carry the motif of

Divine pleasures of paradise

Streamlined through the flow of time

Till I shall someday rise

To greet and hold you in my arms

Just as you would greet and hold

My soul and body; and find our patterns

Cast in the other's mould.

And our lives shall mix and merge together

With insurmountable pleasures lent

By the gifts of nature on this earth

Where our lives were merrily spent.

THE QUERY

Must Your prominence make its presence

Felt when life ebbs out

Like a dwindling lamp with drying fuel

Or a feeble geyser which fails to spout?

Must Your whispers reach the ears

When the ears can no more hear

The sounds of the mortal world beside

And the thunders of fury and of fear?

Must Your shape stand well-defined

When the eyes can no more see

And vision loses its ground on earth

And the soul sinks helplessly?

Why then should Your image not

Transmit itself when the senses are

Clear and vivid in our lives

And not so worn out or bizarre?

Why then should You not descend

And make Your presence felt in us

In the finest hours of our vibrant lives

And spill all doubts from their confined truss?

Why then should You not in fairness

Involve Yourself in our lives

As long as we are strong and healthy

And the spirit is charged with all its drives?

QUESTIONS AND AN ANSWER

When life lies shattered and my grief

Knows no halting bound,

And moments pass with melancholy

Hovering all around,

I need to ask You why You should

Celebrate this dawn

By filling the breeze with the fragrance of

The flowers in my lawn?

I need to question why You must

Fill my home with light

Beamed by the sun throughout the day

And spread by the moon at night?

I need to find out why the clouds

Should burst into rains and showers

And help the little buds today

To blossom tomorrow into flowers?

Much as I feel the sorrows which

Follow a parting death,

I need to find the source of joy

When the birth of a life is set.

I need to explore why the world

Should not also grieve with me

And stop its motions just as I

Wish myself to be?

I need an answer why You should

Find pleasure to hold the reins

Of the massive universe, just now when

Nothing in my life remains?

And that's the time when I can feel

Through the span of the passing age,

The magnitude and the expanse of

Your image,

Which overwhelms, fills and overflows

My seeking human mind

And leaves nothing more to cry aloud

And nothing more to find!

<u>THE QUESTIONS</u>

The songs which I have sung so often

And the words which I have daily spoken—

Have these reached Your ears, O Lord?

Else I'll fret and lie heartbroken.

The tunes which I have chanted while

Doing my earthly rounds—

Have these produced in Your lyre

The subtlest of the sounds?

The works which I have performed and

Dedicated unto You—

Have they found Your blessings, Lord?

Or dumped in Your endless queue?

Have my prayers met their goal

And reached Your lofty throne?

Have You ever treated me

As a fraction of Your very own?

Are You steady, are You ready

To greet me when I leave

The scaffold of this mortal world

Of a mighty make-believe?

Why this quiescence on Your part?

Why this inane gesture, why?

Without Your answers, the question remains:

Who are You and who am I?

QUO VADIS, ROMANCE?

Romance is no more a romance when

Losses rule our lives

And the harshness of the soul erupts

With all its piercing drives;

When, for a moment, we forget

The passion which was the source

Of loving, living and of holding

Each other's hands in the usual course;

When all of a sudden anger wields

Its mighty sharpened sword

And inflicts words quite uncalled for

Which the heat can ill afford;

When expressions are sized to shape

Like an arrow's pointed end

To hit the target flawlessly

With the message to be sent;

When the victim of the rage and wrath

Sheds an unseen tear

Craving a kindlier word or two

From someone who is dear;

When the imprints left on time's footage

Are thrown aside in haste

Leaving no room for condonation

Of failures inadvertent yet chaste;

When understanding melts in the heat of fury

And the feelings are but dry,

When the ear fails to give its audience

To the sound of a wail or a sigh;

When the man is no more a man to reckon

And is no more worth the name—

Romance is no more a romance then

But an apostle of shame.

<u>THE RAINBOW</u>

I have never viewed this life of mine

As I should have done all through

For petty thoughts have obscured all

Better thoughts which grew.

I sold the godly, bought the oddly

Where earthly pleasures made me rue.

I never heard your voice which must

Have had the qualities as of gold,

For sounds of music, loud and thunderous

Have put you calls on hold.

I heard the tuition, lost your fusion

And welcomed miseries most untold.

I have never worshipped as one should

By parting with one's lust,

For my wants and desires as a man

Had always been a must.

Peace I chanted, but wealth I wanted,

Which made my prayers rust.

I have never covered my human flaws

And played a dual role,

For I am what I am and can't

Change myself in part or whole.

I am what I'll always be—that's how you must accept me,

For that's the rainbow of my soul.

THE REBIRTH

When I dance with all my dormant senses

And feelings of my soul,

I find that the solitude in my life

Has reached its golden goal.

And I savour every moment which

Paints my solitary hours

Where the pleasure of knowing my inner self

Over every issue towers.

And my wisdom grows with leaping marches

In the wilderness where I

Am left with nothing but my feelings

Under your blue and open sky:

Feelings that my life is spent

In appreciation of all that's good and nice;

Of all the pleasures showcased through

Your every strange device;

Feelings which have given me

My peace of heart and mind

In the midst of spilling turmoil which

Lies in me entwined;

Feelings which have slowly quietened

The sounds of my cries and wails

And seasoned me with graceful silence

Like that which follows the mighty gales;

Feelings which have nurtured quietly

The essence of the man within

The depth of my living conscience where

Untainted pleasures dance and spin.

Now then shall emerge a newer soul,

Glossy, upright, spic and span

To remind me every moment of

The flowering of a newborn man.

THE REIMBURSEMENT

As I pick up memories one by one

From life's massive field,

And try to assess on my own

What these tend to yield,

My soul draws a total blank

And my mind is filled with awe

To find that nothing, nothing, nothing is

Based on a concrete law.

Tragedy has cast its morbid spell

In life's ripples everywhere,

Where nothing remains on the tracks

Either to retrieve or to share.

And the mind with its frantic earthly efforts

To joyfully survive,

Dwells on incredible absurdities

Of a meaningless counterfeited life.

And hence my woeful mortal motions

Amalgamate with the universe

Where God through all the forms of nature

Embraces me to reimburse

All that I have lost in life,

And all that I have never gained,

Till peace arrives to cleanse the spots

Which fate had badly stained.

<u>REMINDERS</u>

I hear your heart-throbs in the air

Which touch the chords which bind

Our existence now mellowed with

The distance of your mind;

But the rhythms raised in subtle sweetness

In the strings thus struck by sounds

Of beats which pulsate in your heart,

In the wall of my chest resounds.

So it is when the sunrays weave

Magic moments before my eyes

When your floating essence knits your presence

While oblivion in your spirit lies.

So it is when I feel the warmth

Of the passing summer breeze

Which reminds me of the warmth you lent,

Far more pleasing than all of these.

So it is when the showers drop

Like torrents from the heights,

Which remind me of your raining passions

Merged with my heart's delights.

So it is when your mind and feelings

Tend to forget me,

Which reminds me of out welded past

So everlastingly

<u>THE REPLAY</u>

If ever in my life I should

Lose my playing flute,

Let my tears express all my feelings

As the painful substitute.

The monsoon wind shall cry aloud

Moistened by the rains

Wandering in the futile search

Of tunes I've lost in life's terrains.

The sunrays shall but seek to light

All obscure mountain caves;

And every crevice on the endless beach

Shall be filled and explored by the waves—

To find out where the music of

My flute has disappeared,

With which I had in the prime of life,

The entire world endeared.

And in my pains and tears of loss,

I'll turn to You again

To ask You how I could but ever

My missing flute regain.

And You shall stand in glory, Lord,

To lift me in Your arms

And play the reeds of all my senses

To spread Your music with all its charms.

And then the flute I lost in life

Shall resurrect itself through me

Reverberating with the sound of music

In divine ecstasy.

<u>THE RESEARCH</u>

Though every other day which passes

Seems so usual in my view,

Yet every newborn day unfolds

Expectations fresh and new;

And hopes of every shape and order

Find their breeding ground,

And explorations of the strange and unknown

Beckon all around;

And the firsts of sunrays splash their colours

On life's massive span

To spread the message that love and peace

Should reign in the world of man.

Likewise and in the same context,

You seem so common every other day,

Yet when we meet, my first impulse

Is to hold your arms and sway

Together in a world where we

Explore ourselves to seek and find

The strength to move and proceed forward

By breaking the chains which pull behind.

And thus we shall rock in ecstasy

Where divinity and mankind

Lie locked in love and blocked in peace

And rejoice over the priceless find.

THE RESTLESSNESS

What is it that I pine for always

Unknowingly?

And makes me ever so very restless

Within me?

These issues never find their answers

In spite of my endless search,

Leaving me where I had been

With the same old curious urge.

And life shoots out like a falling star

To burn out where it will,

And within the fractioned speck of time,

Craves its desired fill—

The fill of peace, the fill of knowledge,

The fill of satisfying

All that I've been searching for

And for all that I've been sighing.

And throughout this limited span of life

The restlessness shall reign,

To drive my spirit onward to

Reach Your grand domain.

<u>RESUSCITATION OF THE UNCONSCIOUS</u>

The fact that my mind has dwelt on you

At the end of every day

When, exhausted, I tend to rest

After all my work and play,

Lends motion to my heart and soul

Without the slightest strain

To think of you so untiringly

Again, again and all over again.

How strange it is that the mind should be

Obsessed with your thought

And build your shape in front of me

And feel your presence on the spot.

More strange it is to find my mind

Acting on its own

To raise music on its vibrant chords

Unaided and alone,—

The music with which love is bound

And ecstasy finds its gait

And affection is spilled all over

And our emotions are in spate.

Ere I consciously think of you,

You raise your turbulent waves

Through the unconscious part of my existence

Which silently craves

The enlightenment which makes a man

Worthy of his deeds

Through love and passion which every man

Inherently needs.

<u>REVELATION OF THE UNKNOWN</u>

Life is worth living

A hundred thousand times

Through precious moments spent

In destiny's strangest rhymes.

At the turn of every corner

I find there's something new,

Where the unknown reveals itself

And discloses a friend in You.

Every sunrise brings a gift,

Every moonlight, pleasure,

And the subtle presence of Your image

Lends happiness beyond measure.

The entire world is a host

Catering to my needs,

My entire being is a guest

Where divine ecstasy breeds.

And the *Zeitgeist* merges now

As it must and should

With my blissful existence

Combining the bad and the good.

And unto my life is lent

Satisfaction with grace

As I lie amidst nature

In Your embrace.

And that's where my life

Is worth its breath

Till we merge afresh

After my death.

THE REVOLUTION

Rejected by the world at large,

Dejected, my notions lie,

While all my passions exult themselves

With every heaving sigh.

And every pain that's thrust on me

Revels much with joy,

As I find the taste of the pure and genuine

As distinguished from the world's alloy.

This is where my freedom unfolds

Within my mind and conscience, both;

And tears off all those inane shackles

Which withhold the prospects of my growth.

This is where I meet man's challenge

On reason's strange crossroads;

And like a gladiator fighting for a cause,

Cross my swords.

And from every drop of blood which shall

Redden the dust below my feet,

Shall be raised a hundred thousand urges to

Ensure wrong's defeat.

And my freedom shall be won

Through the satisfaction derived of my own,

While I, with my obsessions,

Shall triumph alone.

Let me fill the river of my life

With honeyed freedom to its brink;

Let me celebrate the coronation of

My thoughts as I would like to think.

THE ROLE

Somewhere in my heart and mind,

A note of error breeds;

Somewhere all my existence,

In painful silence bleeds.

Somewhere in my trail of life,

There's the pain of a broken reed;

But there then You are present, Lord,

In my agony, in my need.

From the notes of discord in the music

Played through the lyre of my life,

I seek You out Lord, in my pains,

I see You roam alive.

Thus then break my reeds of life

And strike me with discord,

That I may feel You everywhere,

That I may see You, Lord!

To free me from this bondage and

To cause emancipation of my soul,

Burn me, strike me, let me bleed,

O Lord, my Master, play Your role!

And in course of all my pains endured

Till the day when I shall die,

Bless my soul with the fusion of

Your 'You' and my entire 'I'.

THE ROMANCE

Romance for me with all its charms

Has just begun.

The net of love with its ecstasy

Has just been spun.

For I have turned to You

When the world has failed

To heal my wounds with which

I had ailed.

Here my sense finds boundless joys

In a manner, right and just,

Where I can hold You unobstructed

In divine trust.

Here You grip my soul and spirit

Endlessly

And enhance loves magnitude

To infinity.

And here You draw me close and closer

And absorb all my pains

Till You and I are one and only,

And nothing else remains.

THE ROUTE

Whichever way I turn to seek

Freedom from my ties,

The mirror image of my self

With all its bondage lies.

My lust for the best of mortal cravings

With all its devilish shapes

Stands between my world and yours,

And stares at me and apes.

When I shall disown all I own

And place them at your feet

And forget all my pains and laughter

And in hopelessness retreat;

When I shall earn my poverty

From all the richness of this life;

When I shall lose my friends and still

In the thoughts of their company, thrive;

When I shall carve out peace and content

From the array of my sins

And feel the magic of your silence

Amidst all the sounds and dins;

When I shall forget who am I

And let my spirit roam,

Unnamed, untamed, formless through

'Kshiti, Yap, Teja, Marut, Byom'; (earth, water,fire,air,space)

Then and only then I shall

Find and calmly reach

My much desired world of freedom

And the realm of my peace.

<u>THE SACROSANCT</u>

These moments are but mine alone—

These moments when I pray

And think of You as the only friend

To guard me on my way.

But mockery must not find its place

In worship's holy spot,

For that's the only place where we

Tie our daily knot.

And that's the only time when I

Seek Your kindly light;

That's the only moment when

I see You 'fore my sight.

That's the only platform where

You answer all my cravings, Lord;

That's the only station where

I can mingle with my God.

My poems are temples built by words

Where God His worship finds

And sends His image down to earth

For a meeting of our minds.

Defile not this worship then,

Belittle not my lines,—

For here I've found my divine rest,

And here my lifeline shines.

THE SATIETY

If I had known how to sing,

I would have sung Your praise;

If I had known how to draw,

I would have drawn Your image.

My words find no pomp and décor

Worthy of Your name

In the absence of my songs and drawings

And in the presence of my shame.

What an irony, what a farce,

That I should think of You

Every moment, yet without

The finest possible view.

I have not been blessed with

The arts of the human voice,

Or the subtle fingers with which artists

Immensely rejoice.

For me, the satiety of my soul

Sounds its barren alerts,

For I have nothing in my hold

Save the dryness of my words.

And through my words I convey myself

To the realm where You dwell

And unfold all my feelings there

And sound the worship bell.

And should You receive with Your kindness

The meaning of my words,—

That shall be my cherished, treasured

And lifelong rewards.

THE SATISFACTION

My yesterdays were filled with tears,

My todays are filled with putrid sores;

My tomorrows therefore must be filled

In turn with fortune's golden stores.

In the quicksand of life's desert-lands,

My feet are somewhere stuck;

But I'll lift them soon, for nature's balance

Must be fairly struck.

Destiny was never meant to be

Destined with rigid traits

And travel on a one-way route

All along our fates.

My past has seasoned me in form

To bear my present's weight

With the strength of which I await the future,

For nothing can be ever late.

My tears shall dry, my sores shall die,

My soul shall be lifted high

In praise and glory of my own

Before my last goodbye.

THE SEASONING

When I see life merged in oneness with

The ultimate, that's death,

All concepts of rights and wrongs

Grief and joys and tears and songs

Seem to be wrongly set.

And as I travel along the unknown path

Which fate has paved in life,

The cognizance is lent to me

That my end in death must somewhere be

To crown my onward drive.

And my soul then rises far beyond

All mortal joys and tears

Where the notion of all do's and don'ts

With man-made norms of woulds and won'ts,

Strangely disappears.

There then at the final lap

Where life stands seasoned all the more,

My soul stands refreshed in Your light

Shorn of all that's wrong or right

In the halo of Your divine shore.

<u>SEEK AND YOU WILL FIND!</u>

I marvel at the spread of beauty

Through the dark contours of the night

Where the faint lights of a newborn moon

Quiver by the side

Of floating clouds which softly play

A game of hide and seek,

Now once veiling, then unveiling

The newborn's smiling cheek.

Surrounded here by hushing whispers

Of the caressing breeze which passes

By and lifts up rhythms

Of soft music through the leaves and grasses,

I stand enchanted and thrilled as ever

Just as I had been

Ages ago when I was born

And in my infant eyes had seen

The first rays of the golden sun

And feasted on the sight

Of knowledge, wisdom and erudition

Through the first kiss of light.

Your gifts are scattered everywhere

But I must only breed the eye

To see, to feel and then absorb

Your marvels in my 'I'.

THE SENSE OF RELIEF

In the burden of my work in life,

My longings run along

The unseen linking path where You

Sing Your resonant song

Through the sounds of winds and raging storms

And sounds of raindrops and the seas

And sounds of nature all along

Which never seem to cease.

And the more I am engulfed, Lord,

By the burden of my work,

The more this tired soul of mine

Seeks its resting mark.

In You I find my solace, Lord,

In You I find my peace,

In You lies the end of all my quests,

And the end of all my pleas.

Lord, my Lord, in You alone,

My confidence finds life,

In You alone, my Lord, O Lord,

My soul and being survive.

I wish to tie our hearts together

So that they would never sever;

I wish I could but embrace You

And kiss Your hands forever.

SILENCE UNTO SPEECH

Not a single note of sound I hear

In the entire mountain range;

Not a single note of breeze does stir

As the shimmering colours change

Through yellow, orange, red and crimson

And a host of other hues

As I stand watching with utter awe

These priceless sublime views.

And there You stand then with Your forms

As the silence slowly breaks

While You talk to me from the other end

Of the charming mountain lakes.

And that's the sound I hear right now

Echoing through the hills

Raising its waves through the placid hills

Which now the valley fills.

I hear the sound, I feel the breeze—

And with these I wrap each human sense

To extract the goodness of my soul

By feeling the mighty difference

Between the soundless tracks and the sounds You send

Through tracts so grand and fine

Which tend to convert instantly

The earthly into the divine.

Oh, that I could also convert

My solemn silence into lovely speech

And bring the precious earthly to

The vicinity of the divine reach!

THE SORCERER'S TUNES

All along life's hinterland

The sorcerer plays his tunes,

Beckoning every soul to quit

This desert's fake sand-dunes.

But the melodies from the wizard's wand

Devastatingly fade,

As they find no audience in the world

Which man has himself made.

But the sorcerer spins his magic still

As time flows quietly by,

To enchant every man when he

Should reach the time to die.

For death should taste then sweet indeed

When life is at its end,

While the player of the flute turns out

To be a lifelong friend.

And then the tunes which the sorcerer plays

Their hidden marvels find—

And O! The pleasure!—O! The peace!

To leave the world behind!

THE SOULSEARCHING

Have I ever breathed in fullness

The satiety latent in your airs;

Have I drunk the peace-filled coolness

Of the water stored in the deepest layers?

Have I seen with the widest visions,

The colours concealed in the sun;

Have I felt the mirth and magic

With which life on earth is daily spun?

Have I ever drawn in myself,

The finer feelings of the mind;

Have I ever searched to find

The jewels which lie in me enshrined?

Have I ever prayed in earnest

For the sake of prayers only;

Or absorbed the entire world me

At a time when I felt sad and lonely?

Have I ever scanned with joy,

The moments through which the flowers grow;

Or ever tried to find a friend

Disguised in my bitterest foe?

Have I stared in awe and wonder

At the vastness of the star-filled sky;

And asked to myself a single question:

"Who am I, Oh, who am I?"

Have I likewise gazed aghast

At the endless heavens lost in view:

And enthralled, hurled just one more question:

"Who are You, Oh, who are You?"

SOUNDS OF DISTANT DRUMS

Sounds of distant drums? The parlance weaves

A net of ecstasy, a mystic ambience

Which hold me petrified

And colour my existence

With hopes, aspirations and desires

To know what is unknown;

And to fly towards destinations unexplored

Where none else has ever flown.

And the unseen drumbeats fill the air

And send their throbbing waves

To splash against my entire soul

And extract what it craves.

Nothing inspired me ever before,

Nothing ever fumed

From the grottoes of my life and spirit

From where is now exhumed

The lust to live my life afresh,

The will to strike the tunes again,

The vision to see my inbuilt values,

And the power to rule my own domain.

Here then is a different man

Recreated by the sounds

Of distant drums, where the drummers are

Out of visual bounds.

And as the sounds of drumbeats fade,

Till the ears can no more hear,

Perhaps to some unknown destination

Far away from here,

They leave behind an aura which

Makes my manhood shine

With a radiance left to be treasured and

Equated with all that seems divine.

THE SPIRIT'S SONG

Petals bearing nature's colours

Of pink and white and fawn,

Lie scattered in hundred thousand numbers

All throughout my lawn.

Just as thoughts, a hundred thousand,

Lie scattered throughout my mind,

Where a single thought, all by itself,

Does not lie defined,

But all of them in their entirety,

Make their burden felt

Where the sweetness of my melancholy

Seems to be aptly spelt.

Likewise all these petals render

With their fragrance, soft and raw,

An ambience where divinity stares

At the earthly, with adoration and awe.

Let my earthly inclinations then

Seek out their divine route

From this very place of worship where

My mind plays my spirit's flute.

Every petal, out of a hundred thousand,

Which makes this lawn divine,

Is the provenance where my burdened thoughts

With the godly align.

And I shall spend my life and times

With all my thoughts alone;

And I shall stay with my spirit here

With an aura of my own;

Till someday I shall raise my soul

To merge with You in turn

And together we shall once again

Unto this paradise return.

THE STAND

The world moves on with unchanged rhymes

Preset within both life and death

Where the past, present and the future,

As strange bedfellows, with each other mate;

And whether rolling in wealth and luxury

Or whether morsel-starved,

The destiny of man in rigorous waves

Of uncertain events, is recklessly carved.

Yet nothing shall alter even the least

Where rigidity rules the fate,

For that what shall happen, shall always happen

In certain terms through an uncertain state.

The day is uncertain when it begins

Being fed by the morning rays,

Yet the end is so certain as the events

Fit in smugly in the proper place.

Life is uncertain when it travels

Across its tumultuous rugged course

Till death most certainly intersects

And stops the journey and breaks the oars.

Through the uncertain terrains of my life,

Let me therefore take the stand

That somewhere at the crossroads, I,

More than certain, must understand

My identity as a speck of life

In Your massive universe

To appreciate Your rhyme of contrasts

And Your awful mystic verse.

THE STORY OF AN ORPHAN

My mother died at childbirth, but I,

A wretched child, was born to face

The world without a father, who had fled

And left my mother to disgrace.

Years have passed and I have grown

With the elegance in my blood

Yet with an unknown parentage

And a thousand thoughts which flood

The mind with agony and with pains

Which have kept at bay, my natural bliss,

As I have been deprived from my birth

Of a mother's affection or a father's kiss.

I missed the feelings a child should have

While holding its father's hands,

I missed the shivers a child should feel

While sucking its mother's mammary glands.

I am like a granite with colours showing

And my heart is transformed into stone

And every nerve is petrified

And my walk is all alone.

I have no name, I have no links

To the bloodline where I belong,

And the only bondage is with God

Through my ever mournful song:

The song which is wet with an orphan's tears,

The song which is dry with lovelorn moods,

The song which frets to meet its genesis,

The song which seeks to find its roots;

The song which no man should ever sing,

No man should ever hear,

For it carries the burden of the pain

Which no man should ever bear;

The song which can be only sung

When the ancestry is known

To no one else on earth but only

God and God alone.

Let me sing then, let me sing,

Let me sing my song of pains

And forget that my orphaned birth

Could ever contain stamps of stains.

THE STREET HAWKER

Someone asked me on my way:
'Hey, Street Hawker, what have you in store?'
I said: 'I have stored my love for you,—
Only this and nothing more!'

'Only this and nothing more?
What's the price-tag please?'
'It is priceless,' I said hawking,
The more I give, it'll never cease!'

'Are there strings attached?' he asked.
I said: 'Yes, there are!
When I fill this in your heart and soul,
Distribute this both near and far!'

'Your ware is strange!' he whispered slowly,
'Can you show me how it looks?'
—'I can tell you how it feels,' I said,
But can't demonstrate through picture books.'

'What's the use of hawking love
If no one asks for it?'
'I don't wait for the asking,' said I,
'I just give when I deem it fit.'

'But you shall waste your life like this,'
The stranger said in awe.
I said: 'That's the bliss I find
Through my lifelong flaw.'

'Why do you hawk then with such strain
If your profit is but nil?'
I replied: 'Just because, by this I find
My content and my peaceful fill!'

'You are insane,' said the speaker;
'A worthless, useless guy!'
'Your words are the profits earned,' I said,
Heaving a silent sigh.

THE SURVIVAL

Stranded on the marsh and moors

Across the wastelands of my life,

I find my peace now evermore

In this aimless drift and drive.

Here then all my morbid fear

Crosses all its bounds

Where there is nothing more to fear

And only strength surrounds:

Strength surrounds my entire being,

Strength surrounds my all

And resurrects with pomp and gaiety,

Survival's wherewithal.

Here I hear the call of Apollo

From Delphi's ancient ruins:

'Gnothi se-ow-ton'—'Know thyself'—

For he who knows is he who wins.

In the wilderness of a forlorn life,

The cognizance is lent to me:

In a life mistaken, God forsaken,

I must survive, I must be.

And in the course of bleeding through

The dry and thorny tracts,

I must, par excellence, just for You,

Perform all my acts.

SURYA PRANAM

The sunrays of the newborn year

Cleanse all evils from my thoughts

And unto a better life of happy living,

My hovering soul escorts.

And all my wretched helpless feelings

Are burnt in the glistening rays

Of the rising sun which energises

My passing days.

Let me bask in this refreshed light

And in divine luster, burn,

And let me imbibe in my soul

The strength and power of the sun.

That's my prayer through which my life

Finds its confidence

And ample reasons to beautify

My mortal existence.

That's my prayer through which my soul

Seeks its emancipation

And lifts itself to newer heights

To leave the earthly station.

And that is precisely where

You and I,

Through the annals of eternity,

In fusion, lie.

THE TASTE

How sweet should water taste when I

Quench my arid thirst,

How sweet should peace then taste when I

Need it fast and first.

For in the rapid course of a rugged life,

Things taste sweet indeed,

When necessity with its acute wants

Shows me what I need.

My gratitude, Lord, for having wrecked

My life and fate and time,

Where sweet does taste now more than ever

The nectar of Your crime.

<u>TASTING THE ULTIMATE</u>

As the fading rays of the setting sun

Tranquilise the heat

Of the scorching day,—frustrations

With all their sweetness greet

The lava erupted from the core

Of the desperately seeking soul;

And then darkness descends and painfully joins

Both ends of the pole.

Whatever remains now in the dark

Must be lighted all anew

And the spirit must be raised to heights

Where its status had been due.

Whatever remains obscure now

Has to be seen again

In lights regained from lost horizons

By dispersing the clouds and rain.

Whatever mistakes had been made

Through emotions in the past

Must be reviewed with the notion

That these do never last.

Who should then now give me strength?

Who should then now hold my hands?

Who should lead me through the deserts

And show the footmarks on the sands?

I wait here on my earthly platform,

Alone and lonely, for that power

Which brought me life at my natal moments

And shall meet me at my fatal hour.

This waiting tastes so grand and charming

As my entity blossoms like a flower

And ushers in the finest magic

Of living through each breathing hour.

And through the genesis of the long-lost pains,

Life explores the finest;

And gifts to itself all the pleasures

Extracted from the divinest.

THE TEACHER

Satan has its grotesque hideouts

On the terrains of my fate

To backstab all my efforts to

Find You as my mate.

And as a wanderer in thirst and hunger

Roams in the desert lands

And seeing a mirage, loses tracks

Ere he understands,—

I lose my way while searching for

The worthless shine I see

In earthly matters, bright and sparkling,

Which the Devil offers me.

And then when the misconception

Loses all its hues,

And I learn the meaning of this life

From all its painful views,—

I turn around to face the Devil

Either to curse or thank,

But find instead, Your godly image

In the first and foremost rank.

THE THANKSGIVING

My words have drifted far away

Tonight in your skies

To find their audience in the world

Where no one ever dies,

But lives forever in Your arms

Distanced from the strife

Which draws the blood of man by man

And blasts the human life.

What then should I ask of You,

What then should I pray

Through the words which convey all my passions

And express all I wish to say?

I wish to whisper in Your ears

My thanks for all the pains You've gifted,

For that's the massive source through which

My peace in life is lifted.

I wish to offer through my words

My thanks for all the joys You've lent,

For that's the source through which the meaning

Of pain is amply sent.

My words shall never exhaust themselves

Until their mission ends

By thanking You for joys and sorrows

Where life so gracefully blends

With death; and where indeed

The mortal chain lies bent and broken

To be lifted and be set again

With newer words which are not yet spoken.

THE "OM"

In the endless expanse of eternal time

Where both the unknown and the known

Merge in cosmic rhyme and rhythm

With a fine-tuned subtle tone,

Oh, The Shapeless! Oh, the Formless!

All pervasive, all engulfing 'Om'!

Draw my soul and spirit in

The bay of peace and lead me home!

Lead me home where truth and light

Drive all ills away;

Lighten up my course and track

Lest I miss and lose my way.

The sound's the sound of flute and thunder,

The soft and sturdy 'Om',

Reverberating through the universe

Where I must find my home.

The streams of blood which hold my life

Gush and swirl and foam

Like rushing rivers from the mountains,

When I hear the sound of 'Om'.

The omnipotent, the omniscient,

Oh! The omnipresent 'Om'!

Enlighten my all in your magnificence

And lead me safely home!

THE QUESTION—THE ANSWER

As I walked with him, he pointed out

That my shirt was torn

And my shoes had holes; and made it clear

That I was an object of his scorn;

That I was a wretch on whom he could

Spend his heartiest laugh;

That I was a nincompoop whom he could treat

With sheer rebuff.

To me, however, this mattered little,

For I knew that richness lay

In acceptance of the facts of life

And of destiny which changes every day.

As such I harnessed all my pains

Which from such words arose

Lest they swell and vibrate in my mind

And their reflections on my face impose.

Thinking thus, I parted ways

And traveled on my own,

Till age had grown on both of us

And seasoned the marrow in our bone.

And then one day we met again

After the expiry of our living span

When our existence was long forgotten

In the mortal world of man.

I asked him if he had any questions left

To be answered all the more:

My friend, of course, then failed to find

Any questions on this score.

For we were spirits shorn of shapes,

Or for that matter, shoes and shirts,

Where nothing really has a meaning

And nothing really hurts.

My friend then saw through what I drove at

And realized the error made

When he had walked with me down there

And questioned my tattered state.

THOU ART!

I know that in my times of need

Somehow You are there,

Somewhere in the hiding where

My thoughts hardly dare.

And when the crisis ripens and

Takes a fearful shape,

And the devil himself gags and blocks

All my outlets of escape—

Something happens out of nothing

And the darkness moves away

To show me the source from where the light

Emits its hopeful ray.

And I can breathe then freely, Oh!

I can breathe Your scent,

I can feel Your hiding place

In my mortal existence.

And in the midst of all my chaos,

Disorders, strife and pains,

My life is beautified and the charm to live

Ever always remains.

<u>**TO MY SOUL**</u>

In the discreet silence of these woods, listen quietly!

Listen quietly to the music of your heart

And the rhythms of life shall reveal themselves

Like a neatly spread-out chart.

Here you'll hear the softer sounds

Of leaves which fall like sudden showers

With gusts of winds which strike the trees

Off and on through the passing hours.

Here you'll hear the sounds of ripples

Of the watery stretch around

And the sounds your footsteps raise while walking

Quietly on the grassy ground.

Here in silence, all by yourself,

You can converse with your mind

And merge yourself in a thousand thoughts

Of moments left behind.

Here you'll find that silence is

Not silence in the least

For you shall revel in the sounds of silence

On which your craving soul shall feast.

Here you'll find that solitude

Has no painful tales to tell,

For here you'll never feel alone

Amidst sound's magic spell.

It all depends on how you convert

Life's events into shape

And with the trophy of your golden moments

Happily escape.

TO THE DEVASTATED

When destiny plays havoc with your life

And chaos and discords blur

All that's lovely, bright and hopeful

And all that's grand and *wunderbar,*—

Then's the time to lift your soul

To high and higher grounds,

Then's the time to see His visions

And hear His blissful sounds.

Then's the time to search for peace,

Then's the time to cast your doubts

On the worth you've imposed so long on

Your earthly whereabouts.

Then's the time to understand

The self which lies in you,

And be the judge and jury, both,

Of your own review.

Then's the time to equate yourself

To divinity's greater cause

And merge with Godhead's omnipotence

And voice your own applause.

Then's the time to reach beyond

Mortality's defined bounds

And touch the domain where eternity

Your life surrounds.

Then's the time to weave the garland

Of pains and laughter, both,

And place them at His feet, discarded,

And simply sing His ode.

And then's the time

To forever cross

The barriers of your grief and joy

And your mortal gains and loss.

<u>TO THE MIND</u>

Think beyond, Mind, think beyond

The world of your woes and cross

The mortal barriers which hold you down

By reminding you of your pains and loss.

Think beyond your human feelings

Grounded in the earth;

Think beyond the age-old notions

Of death and birth.

Think beyond the exuberance

Of happiness and of sorrow;

Think beyond yesterday, today

And the unforeseen tomorrow.

Think beyond the reconciliation

Of what you have and haven't got;

Think beyond the comparisons

Between life's brightest and the darkest spot.

Think beyond the distance 'tween

What you own and what you don't;

Think beyond the results of

What you would and what you won't.

Think beyond love and affection

As well as greed and hate;

Think beyond your acquired manhood

And the devastations of fate.

Think beyond the chapters which

You wish to open in your life;

Think beyond the chapters which

Are closed forever, while you survive.

Think beyond the world of the living

And the world of the buried dead;

Think beyond all worldly thoughts

Right from A to Z.

Think beyond the tragic difference

Of wasteful feasting and painful fasting;

Think beyond the human concepts

Of the momentary and the everlasting.

Think beyond all these, restless Mind,

Think beyond all these, and release—

Release yourself in the universe

And find at last your peaceful ease!

<u>TO YOU</u>

While thinking of you in silent motions

Through the quiet hours of the night,

I find my peace, I find my home,

I find my heart's delight.

There I wish my rest should be,

There I crave my grand repose,

There I feel I should have started

And there I wish my last day shows.

The feeling makes the night which passes,

Decked with the colours which I lost

In life; but resurrected now with your advent

Where the better side of fate was tossed.

And now this morning, I am still

Overwhelmed and held

By thoughts of you, which through last night,

Divine luster spelt.

And this is how Lord, every morning,

The day inevitably begins for me,

When I draw within my self and soul

Your thoughts like a madman's spree:

Till the night descends, and I in silence

Again wrap my soul and all,

With thoughts of you in peace and quietness

To fill my spirit's vacant hall.

THE TOUCH OF CLASS

When You wound me hard and make me bleed

To cry aloud in pains,

Your touch of class, O Lord, my Lord!

The touch of class remains.

And just as lightning strikes the earth

And burns all on its way,

In Your wrath and fury, O mighty Power!

Burn my evils everyday.

And in the glow of burning evils,

Let me see my 'I',

And understand and feel in earnest

My life before I die.

TRANSFORMATION? REALLY?

I come here oft to see these mortals

Cleanse themselves by shedding tears

While I wait and observe the serene moments

Where no one interferes

And questions me why my soul adores

The flames of burning pyres

Or steals even a glance to wonder

Why I stare in awe at the dancing fires.

This I feel is the finest temple

Where God is worshipped as well as feared;

Where life with the blood of morbid death,

Is besmeared.

Where man understand life

Through the appreciation of death,

And for a moment allows death to cover

Life's length and breadth;

Where wars and cross-fires seem to be

Ignored and forgotten

And enmity and hatred between man and man

Are treated as putrid and rotten;

Where doubts are raised as to why at all

Man should kill his kind;

And whether this place is an oasis of peace

Which one could really find.

And a hundred thousand words and thoughts

Of erring human acts

Are put to trial on the touchstone of

Some simple basic facts

Of love, sympathy and truthfulness

Between man and man

Where ill feelings, hatred and jealousy

Are outcasts with a complete ban—

And the world seems sweeter than before

Where the earth its paradise earns,

Only to be forgotten and given a go-by

As soon as man leaves this place and home returns.

THE TRUST

Somewhere in the undulations

Of my chequered life,—

Somewhere on the roadside

Of this endless, aimless drive,—

Somewhere in my heart and mind

Where lonesome feelings thrive,—

Somewhere You have crept in silence

To keep me still alive

With the divine touch of love and passion

Besmeared on the scars

Left behind by vexing ravages

Ushered in by ill-timed stars.

And the more I feel Your touch in life

To smoothen all that's odd,—

The more I put my trust in You

And the more I trust in God!

THE TUNES OF DEATH

When my spirit sings the tunes of death

Which seem to be painfully finest,

The tunes of life start dancing with

Rhythms which are the divinest.

And ensconced in that psychic aura

My soul shall rest and resign

And find its peaceful fructification

Across destiny's strange design.

Through the thunderbolts and blasts of life,

My spirit seems to be ever leaning

On the region of that ecstasy

To explore this existence's meaning.

And the exploration never ends but fills

My entire frame with charming powers

To overcome my pains and trauma

Along the bleeding path of passing hours.

And one by one, through my mortal span

As I cross each troubled tear-filled station,

My expectation rises high and higher

To find your glorious manifestation.

THE TWILIGHT'S MAGIC

When the sun is about to depart

And descends in the West,

And the fading twilight communicates

A sense of nature's rest,

I scatter all my restless thoughts

All throughout the reddened skies

And apply them like vermilion

Where God's great forehead lies,

Stretching from the four great corners

And forming the massive dome

Where the boundaries of our lives and deaths

Lose their logic and syndrome;

Where clouds are formed and rainbows painted,

And stars are studded with Your powers,

And heaven's nectar sheds its load

As dewdrops on earth's blossoming flowers.

And on that spread of divine luster,

My restless thoughts are cast

To extract from my existence

The pains which drape my past.

And one by one these thoughts of mine

Are drawn into Your godly glow

Where tranquility soothes my mortal pains

And returns them to me below.

THE UNBOUNDED

As twilight dawns on life's skyline
And motion slows its pace,
The germs of all my undone works
Like monster's on the crust, surface.
They flood my mind and stud my soul
With violent urges from behind
And whip and prod me just to move
And complete all that's undefined.
And my entire spirit tends to rush
And race with the flowing time
Just to find my flesh and bones
Can no more match the rhyme.
No more can they find their rhythms
Tuned to the speeding hours,
No more can they find their strength
Like drooping, withered flowers.
While the mind with all its forward gears
Attempts the fastest moves,
The bones get stuck with weakened joints
In the slush and muddy grooves.

And then I find my inner self

Float out through my stagnant frame

To create a dreamland on this earth

And end this irksome ghastly game.

THE UNEXPLORED

You have gifted me with the plenitude

Which life deserves

And filled up every nook and corner

With the finest of Your grand reserves.

But I have had to plough my way

Through hardened soil and rough terrains

And waste Your gifts while battling through

The starboard and the larboard lanes.

I've missed the mainstream of my life

And unto myself, have done a crime

Where suffixes and prefixes meaninglessly

Have stolen my golden time.

And the nucleus of my life and soul

Remains unexplored, Lord, unexplored,

Where I've never found the time to taste

The honey You have poured.

I've never scanned my inner beauty

Which You wanted me to see;

And I've never found the time to feel

Your existence in me!

THE UNIVERSAL HOME

Nothing fascinates me more than myself

When I equate myself with the universe

And feel in me Your massive spasms

Where the joys of life rehearse.

From dust indeed, I must have been

Raised, and with that very dust

Must I someday amalgamate,

For return home I must.

And that explains why my entire home

Is spread out everywhere

In grains of earth, in drops of water

And rays of light and air.

I am here and all throughout

The length and breadth of Yours,

And step where You step, roam where You roam,

As long as this life endures.

Likewise in the afterworld,

My existence shall find

Its rightful place in the very home

Which life, for me designed.

While living, I must therefore colour

Every speck of dust and earth

And sweeten every drop of water

And accept life with all its worth.

Thus therefore I'll beautify

My massive endless home where we

Can dwell together, dance together,

And forever together be.

THE VALUE OF ZERO

Heaps of slumber load my eyes

While I play riot with my only thought,

Trying to figure what I received

And what I never got.

At the end when I am just about

To fall asleep and quit

The daylong strains of tired limbs

Which sound the Sleep-God's writ,—

I reach the results of the sums

Which tell me that I have not

Received what was due to me

Or that which I never got.

And now you find that either way

You look at it, my dear,

My life has always stuck to zero

And lost its driving gear.

And that perhaps is the graceful place

Where my aspirations never ache,

For I have nothing to lose and nothing to gain,

Nothing to give and nothing to take.

I close my eyes now, deep in peace,

And fall asleep with an empty mind,

Unperturbed by brooding thoughts

Which now are briskly shoved behind.

VIS-À-VIS

As I try to foresee what should happen

To me in the years ahead,

And what should mark my living years

Before I am gone and dead,

A rainbow rises with all its colours

In the shape of God's envoy

From where I decipher in certain terms

The message of hope and joy.

In the motions of the world I find

My pleasures to the brim

And a hundred thousand reasons to

Be grateful to Him.

In the countenance of every man,

I find my self imposed,

And in the pains and joys of every soul,

I find my own endorsed.

My pains are not my pains alone,

And my pleasures are exclusively not my own

If I am to share these with all others

And discard them and thus disown.

THE VISION

The vision haunts me, where I find

My body lying with flowers strewn;

The vision passes soon but leaves

A dismal thread which finely weaves

The chart of my journey's end—

Soon, too soon!

It seems it's twilight; the sun is sunk;

Yet time-wise, life has just crossed noon,

Burdened with questions which unanswered lie

In the mystic fabric of 'how' and 'why';

Now the unceasing search must stop—

Soon, too soon!

Fate, not endeavours; Providence, not manhood,

Rule life; with life they are intimately sewn.

At every step they play their ghastly game

And decide on your failure or your fame

And make a wreck of your manhood—

Soon, too soon!

Time beckons me by the hour

To welcome death as a disguised boon,

Where lifelong agonies find their end

And all my elements merge and blend

To seek their aspired tryst with You—

Soon, too soon!

THE VOICE WITHIN

I must talk to myself now

And converse with my inner voice

And feel the rhythms of the sounds

Which within my soul, rejoice.

Silence in the world around,

Silence in my tongue,

As I speak by myself to a world

Where songs are never sung;

But the melodies of such unsung songs

Float to be picked up by

A tinge of grief, a thrust of sadness,

A drop of tear or a sound of a heaving sigh.

There then I must converse now

With Him who sits within

And tear apart all notions of

My goodness or my sin,

For I am no more what I am

And what I've been before,

For now I am what I am now

After opening my inner door

Where I can talk to myself and

Discard my other sheen

And throw aside the mockery of

What I once had been.

THE VOICE

I've heard the plangent voice within

Ringing through my soul

Like sounds of bells and white conch-shells

Which auspiciously toll,

And remind me that there's a link

Somewhere in between

Man's charted lot and the course of God

On the universal screen.

With this knowledge, I shall sail

And find all regions new

And keep aside life's adverse tide

And evils from my view.

I shall feel the strength in me

Stored through all my births,

With an immense power, every hour

Along life's scattered berths.

I shall never fail or despair

In the worst of pungent times;

I'll rise to face life's toughest phase

In the darkest of the climes.

While the earth may waste its golden hours

In useless noise and din,

I shall hear with an open ear

Your voice of peace which rings within.

<u>WAITING IN ANTICIPATION</u>

In course of life, in an empty train

As I cross each lonely station,

The only feeling which strikes my soul

Is of devastation.

Reveling in the strange domain

Where adversities reverberate

Stultifying my human efforts

To override this morbid state,

I spend these hours of my life

In confrontation of the worst

Which slowly ushers in Your presence

With the understanding of the universe.

And here I am then, face to face

With life and death and You,

Where grief and pleasure, both of these

Disappear from my view.

In readiness I stand here all alone

To encounter that massive power

Which gifted me both life and death

And joy and agony every hour.

Far beyond the mortal regions

Of heartbreaks, joys and tears,

Of gains and losses, hopes and despairs,

Of fearlessness and fears,

Let me find and feel my strength

In an aura of my own

And wait with curious anticipation

Of that what is yet unknown.

THE WALKING

I feel like walking through the path

Flanked by fields of corn

And fill my lungs with the freshness of

The air and sunshine of this morn.

The path goes winding all along

The distance I can see

And melts and mixes far away

To find its rest and lee.

Now I know, as soon as I

Shall cover the entire length

Of the path which reaches simply nowhere

Till I find and reach the other end,

My anxieties shall soon then disappear

And my deliberations shall then cease,

For by then I shall have slowly gathered

My strength of mind and peace.

Thus walk I must midst nature's bounties,

Walk I must in joy,

For in every breath I inhale here,

There's a reason to enjoy.

But my walk is endless like the path,

Yet end it shall some day,

Somewhat tiring, yet inspiring

My soul all the way.

WANDERER IN THE DESERT-LANDS

Wanderer in the desert-lands

In search of deceptive wealth!

When, Oh when must all your ice

Of mortal obsessions melt?

Wanderer in the desert-lands!

I am following you as well,

For I am also a wanderer

In this paradise of hell.

Wanderer, Oh listen to me,

Stop! Stop, for heaven's sake!

In this wilderness of the living dead,

Our lives are held at stake.

Wanderer, Oh! If you don't

Care to hear and halt

And if you wish to take my words

With just a grain of salt,—

Wanderer, then give me time

To reach you and to hold

And grip your hands to pull you back

From the world of the deceptive gold!

Wanderer in the desert-lands!

Feel and inhale the simple breeze

And let the earth throb in your bosom

And return! Oh, return to priceless peace!

WASTE OF TIME?

If gazing at the world is by

Any means a waste,

Let me gaze for hours long

And feel Your divine taste.

Let me stare at the open sky

And the expanse of the fields;

Let me stare at the rainbow's end

And find out what it yields.

Let me stare with awe and wonder

At the ocean's unceasing waves

And the endless marine margin where

The beauty of the sun undrapes.

Let me watch the life around,

Let me gaze at the mountain heights;

Let me absorb in my heart

Nature's sensuous grand delights.

Let me forget my work and art

And gaze at those of Yours

Till my soul its lust and yearnings for

Unreal things abjures.

THE WEBSITE

Surfing on the internet?

Such pleasures are not mine;

For I surf with pleasures where senses are

Superbly divine.

I surf where all my wishes seem

To find their finest place,

Far more sensuous, far more thrilling

Than what man terms as cyberspace.

For me, my password is Your name

Strewn along my life

Like honey-drops with which the bees

Fill the empty hive.

Surfing elsewhere is not my game

For I have filled my soul indeed

With the honey of Your love and name

Where all my pleasures breed.

And thus I'll thrive; and thrive I shall

With thoughts which travel through

My heart and mind to seek and find

You and only You!

THE WORSHIP MODE

My worship unto You is through

My feelings every day

When I send my soul to search for You

In my own humble way.

And the soul returns to say that it

Has failed to find You out;

But I then send my soul again

To do the roundabout.

Thus every day I search for You

With aimless, goal-less strides

Which keep me thinking of Your glory

Through all these psychic rides.

Thus every day I learn of Your

Notions, good or bad,

Which sometimes make me happy and

Sometimes somewhat sad.

And every moment is a moment of

Asking 'how' and 'why'?

With the everlasting exercise

Of 'seek' and 'try'!

And in course of all these deliberations,

Unknowingly I find

That I have worshipped You throughout

In my heart and mind!

And that is how I worship You

Every moment, every day,

By covering me with thoughts of You

In all my work and all my play.

And this is how I tie myself

With passion's greatest urge

Where all Your images lift themselves

And in one whole Godhead merge!

A WINTER NIGHT

It's well past midnight and the night

Is bathed in icy air

As I roam alone and give in coolly

To nature's winter care.

It's quiet and silent all around

And there's not a soul in sight,

For all have crept in cozy beds

To pass this winter night.

But I don't have a wink of sleep

As thousand thoughts arise

To keep me awake till I find the spot

Where the source of all the worries lies.

The more I think or fret or brood,

The more these cancers breed

And eat into my life and soul

And make my arteries bleed.

But the coolness of the winter breeze

Acts like a wonder-balm

And ushers in with grace and elegance,

My much required peace and calm.

It spreads its caress all across

My regions charred with burning scars

As I stand freezing in the cold tonight

Below the kingdom of the twinkling stars.

Shall then my aspired peace and calm

Descend when I'll feel thus cold,

When death shall ask my life to quit

My putrid mortal hold?

Shall the coolness in my death

Act like a wonder-balm

When my soul shall be lifted from my body

To touch Your beckoning arm?

Shall death, in its elegance, caress me

Like the cold and freezing winter breeze?

And cool my unhealed burns and scars

And lay my mind to rest in peace?

<u>2000–2001</u>

I never sensed the time which changed

The last year to the newborn next,

Save and except that You were here

Merged with my working text.

More than ever, more than always,

It's time for me to learn

That no one else but You are only

My most beloved one.

The vacuum in my lonesome life

Is not a vacuum when

I feel Your stately existence

Fill my narrow glen.

Were You here? Oh yes, You were!

For You had led me on

To perfect all my work and art

While a year had come and gone.

And there I stood quite oblivious

While the last year drifted by:

And unkissed by a single soul

When the new year touched the sky.

And the cognizance then dawned on me

That a lonely life is a marvel where

I work to forget all but You

And I work to reach You there!

THIEVES, LIARS, HYPOCRITES, OPPORTUNISTS AND LOVERS

THIEVES of a first class order
stealing time stealthily
from society's time-bound norms
and trespassing into the amphitheatre of prohibitions
followed by lurking risks and dangers
of being ceremoniously unmasked
and losing the veil of a lofty social image.

LIARS, wearing the black robe of falsehood
projected as the garb of truth;
suppressing facts and deceiving the world
surreptitiously cooing around restaurants
cafes and discotheques of the city
or available nooks and corners of rugged lanes
or in the seats of streamlined limousines or ramshackles.

HYPOCRITES of sterling quality
like scaramouchs ruling the stage
with scholarly jargons and logistic precepts
woven into magic which vanishes naturally
in course of being served along the anastomosis
of truths, lies, half-truths and half-lies
pounding conscience into smithereens.

OPPORTUNISTS of the vilest nature
ready like sharp-eyed hungry vultures
to pounce upon the unethical, the immoral,
the polluted and putrid moments
discarded by the general standards of civilization
and shunned by the pious and the holy
as life flows along.

LOVERS, surfing on passionate emotions
of love—genuine, gentle and unadulterated
and unaffected by the poison spouted
by fabrications of man, find sense
in being oblivious of the artificial futility
of the surroundings; and kiss and embrace each other
unlike thieves, liars, hypocrites and opportunists
and render an effective meaning
to life, living and God. Always!